AMERICAN POETS PROJECT

The American Poets Project
is published with a gift in memory of
JAMES MERRILL

Walt Whitman

selected poems

harold bloom editor

AMERICAN POETS PROJECT

THE LIBRARY OF AMERICA

The paper used in this publication meets the minimum requirements of the American National Standard for Information Sciences—Permanence of Paper for Printed Library Materials, ANSI Z39.48—1984.

Design by Chip Kidd and Mark Melnick.

Library of Congress Cataloging-in-Publication Data:
Whitman, Walt, 1819–1892.
[Poems. Selections]
Selected poems / Walt Whitman ; Harold Bloom, editor.
p. cm. — (American poets project ; 4)
Includes index.
ISBN 1-931082-32-4 (alk. paper)
I. Title: Walt Whitman. II. Bloom, Harold. III. Title. IV. Series.
PS3203.B624   2003
813'.3 — dc21
2002032124

10 9 8 7 6 5 4 3 2 1

Walt Whitman

CONTENTS

INTRODUCTION

I

One always wants to start out fresh with Walt Whitman, and read him as though he never has been read before. It is now nearly 150 years since the first appearance of *Leaves of Grass* (1855), but Whitman, like Shakespeare in this one regard, tempts me to confront greatness directly, as though I could be alone with his work. Ben Jonson, introducing the Shakespeare First Folio (1623), writes with a new fervor about his deceased friend and rival, perhaps because he has just read many of the plays for the first time. Ralph Waldo Emerson, responding to Whitman's gift of the first *Leaves of Grass*, triumphantly proclaimed the advent of the American poet he had prophesied. Jonson and Emerson point the way: try to read as though you were Adam early in the morning:

> As Adam early in the morning,
> Walking forth from the bower refresh'd with sleep,

> Behold me where I pass, hear my voice, approach,
> Touch me, touch the palm of your hand to my body
>   as I pass,
> Be not afraid of my body.

"Where I pass," "as I pass": "pass" is one of the superb Whitmanian tropes, and partly indicates his identification with a resurrected Adam-Christ figure, not Jesus but Walt. *First* Walt resurrected, and *then* Whitman died, on March 26, 1892, not yet 73. One might date Walt's resurrection as 1854, when he was in the middle of the journey:

> In vain were nails driven through my hands.
> I remember my crucifixion and bloody coronation
> I remember the mockers and the buffeting insults
> The sepulchre and the white linen have yielded
>   me up
> I am alive in New York and San Francisco,
> Again I tread the streets after two thousand years.
> Not all the traditions can put vitality in churches
> They are not alive, they are cold mortar and brick,
> I can easily build as good, and so can you:—
> Books are not men—

That became, with many changes, section 38, "Song of Myself," but I quote here from the early Notebook version. "Books are not men—," and Whitman has come alive again to replace the Bible, not with a book, but with a man, just as Jesus replaced Scripture for the early Christians. *Leaves of Grass* is the Newest Testament, at least for those who identify the spirit with the American literary imagination.

Though Whitman was raised in a Quaker family (of a dissident variety, following the preacher Elias Hicks), the poet was never a Christian. He can be regarded as the poet proper of what I think may yet be called the American religion, which is post-Christian (though few will admit this). Pentecostalists, Mormons, and Emersonians (among others) have little or no continuity with European Protestantisms. Their ancestry is elsewhere, with heretical strains of Enthusiasm, Hermeticism, and Neo-Platonism. Whitman, though inspired by Emerson, was eclectic and more of an Epicurean materialist than a Transcendental idealist.

Whitman's originality was not conceptual, as Emily Dickinson's was. She had thought everything through again for herself, and employed traditional diction, including theological, in order to subvert it. I can think only of William Blake, and on the highest level, Shakespeare, as comparable to Dickinson in conceptual independence. Whitman, like Wallace Stevens after him, or Tennyson in his own time, is a great poet of nuance, of the inflection of sensations and perceptions, of "the hum of thoughts evaded in the mind" (Stevens). Christ is a thought evaded in Walt Whitman's mind. Like the poet-critic John Hollander, I find that Whitman's poetry looks easy but is very difficult. Criticism, of all varieties, has been largely defeated by Whitman, and the currently fashionable stuff—Foucault-historicist, "Homosexual Poetic," Bio-Determinist—is only another impasse. Whitman demands, and rewards, preternaturally close reading, the kind that I believe is allied to possession-by-memory. You have to know his major poems intimately to render them justice, or for them to alter you, at least as a reader.

Whitman, with only Dickinson as near-rival, is the great American poet, but merits an even higher accolade. He is the principal writer that America—North, Central, or South—has brought to us. Besides Dickinson, the other possible rivals—Emerson, Melville, Henry James,

Faulkner—finally become satellites in the presence of Walt Whitman. Much the same is true of Paz, Neruda, Borges, García Márquez, Lezama Lima, Carpentier, Hispanic-Americans in the wake of Whitman. To be the central writer of the Western Hemisphere, the Bard of the Evening Land, places Walt Whitman as the New World's answer to Europe. Milton, Goethe, Wordsworth, Victor Hugo, Manzoni are Whitman's peers, but none of them matches his immediacy. He will not allow himself to be mediated. The American poets who fled him—Pound and Eliot—came home to him, in ways more profound than they seemed to apprehend.

D. H. Lawrence, fighting hard so as not to be drowned in Whitman, called Walt a "fearfully mistaken" American Moses, a preacher of ALLNESS, yet Lawrence testified that Whitman was the only pioneer poet, breaking a new road ahead into the wilderness. One wants (with reverence) to alter Lawrence's tribute: Whitman seems to me, now, the poet who saved the Western tradition of imaginative literature. Even our most exuberant Resenters cannot dismiss Whitman as another of the Dead White European Males. He is as dead as Shakespeare, or as Dickens. Walt Whitman renewed in his strongest poetry the image of the human as the shoreline where nature and the fantasy-making power collide.

2

The American crisis-poem was stationed by Whitman at the shifting point where beach and sea meet. American poets have followed him there in order to compose what James Wright termed "the shore-ode." This original genre has many distinguished exemplifications, from Wallace Stevens' "The Idea of Order at Key West" and *The Auroras of Autumn* on through meditations by Hart Crane,

John Brooks Wheelwright, Elizabeth Bishop, May Swenson, Amy Clampitt, and A. R. Ammons, as well as others. The shore-ode may be considered as the American equivalent of the English crisis-ode of Wordsworth, Coleridge, Shelley, Keats, and Tennyson, which culminates in the Anglo-Irish W. B. Yeats. The crisis concerns the poet's ability to write the next major poem. William Empson, contemplating Hart Crane's desperate gamble to stay alive, *if the next poem worked*, grimly observed that poetry thus became "a mug's game." That seems about right to me, if you consider Whitman's crucial poems besides "Song of Myself": "The Sleepers," "Crossing Brooklyn Ferry," "As I Ebb'd with the Ocean of Life," "Out of the Cradle Endlessly Rocking," "When Lilacs Last in the Dooryard Bloom'd." Whitman has everything riding on those five poems, like a high-stakes gambler going for broke. Wallace Stevens, who did not like the Whitman tramp-persona, a menace to Stevensian gentility, nevertheless also bets the house on a sequence of shore-odes ultimately as imaginatively desperate as Hart Crane's "The Broken Tower."

Whitman is the genius of the shores of America, to which he said Emerson had led him. One wishes that Whitman had achieved homoerotic fulfillment, but the evidence indicates otherwise. His temperament was profoundly autoerotic, and his most original trope, the "tally," shows that he speaks proudly for Onan. My intentions in this essay are formalistic and not polemical: close reading is what Whitman more than ever requires.

3

"Song of Myself," untitled and undivided into sections in 1855, is the heart of Walt Whitman as Kosmos. But which Walt Whitman? The poem relies upon a tripartite division of the psyche: two selves and a soul, where the soul is the problematic entity. One self dominates the title: song of myself, not song of the real me or me myself, let alone song of the soul. In the second *Leaves of Grass* (1856), the title became: "A Poem of Walt Whitman, an American." Section 24 identified this American as:

> Walt Whitman, a kosmos, of Manhattan the son,
> Turbulent, fleshy, sensual, eating, drinking and
>   breeding . . .

In 1855, "myself" is "Walt Whitman, an American, one of the roughs." This outward persona, the rough Walt, is the poem's protagonist, but it is not alone. So original is Whitman's psychic cartography or map of the mind that I am tempted to call it a pneumatology of sorts, since Whitman's selves are not part of nature, while the Whitmanian soul, like the body, is. Emerson's "The Over-Soul" "is that great nature in which we rest," while the self of his "Self-Reliance" is "the aboriginal Self," preceding nature and as old as God. Whitman begins with this Emersonian gnosis but, unlike Emerson, he is aware of two selves. One is the rough American, too overtly male and aggressive. The other is a quasi-feminine "real me" or "me myself," uneasily akin to the fourfold image of night, death, the mother, and the sea, that ultimately represents Whitman's soul. If Whitman's soul is natural, it is a nature alienated from his "real me." Emerson's "soul" and "self" emerge from the European rhetorical tradition, where soul is ethos or character, and self is pathos or personality. Ethos is action, pathos is suffering, but Whitman tends to be estranged from his character or soul, a nature not known to him, a suspicious blank. Since Whitman's rough persona moves through a bewildering series of synecdoches, or part-for-whole symbols, neither we nor Whitman have much knowledge of it. The me myself, Whitman knows very well: his real me is a genius at knowing, and being known.

One of the most beautiful and influential passages in "Song of Myself" is section 4:

> Trippers and askers surround me,
> People I meet, the effect upon me of my early life
>> or the ward and city I live in, or the nation,
> The latest dates, discoveries, inventions, societies,
>> authors old and new,
> My dinner, dress, associates, looks, compliments,
>> dues,
> The real or fancied indifference of some man or
>> woman I love,
> The sickness of one of my folks or of myself, or
>> ill-doing or loss or lack of money, or
>> depressions or exaltations,
> Battles, the horrors of fratricidal war, the fever of
>> doubtful news, the fitful events;
> These come to me days and nights and go from
>> me again,
> But they are not the Me myself.
>
> Apart from the pulling and hauling stands what
>> I am,
> Stands amused, complacent, compassionating,
>> idle, unitary,
> Looks down, is erect, or bends an arm on an
>> impalpable certain rest,
> Looking with side-curved head curious what will
>> come next,
> Both in and out of the game and watching and
>> wondering at it.

> Backward I see in my own days where I sweated
> > through fog with linguists and contenders,
> I have no mockings or arguments, I witness and
> > wait.

How marvelous that "Me myself" is! It is "compla-
cent" in the older sense only, desiring to please, rather
than self-satisfied, and though unitary, this is the fusion of
the androgyne. Incredibly graceful, arm bent on that oxy-
moronic "impalpable certain rest," the real me anticipates
a stance that haunts American poets from T. S. Eliot to
John Ashbery:

> Looking with side-curved head curious what will
> > come next,
> Both in and out of the game and watching and
> > wondering at it.

This is "the other I am," not the "I" of "Song of
Myself." The most enigmatic lines in the poem follow, to
start section 5:

> I believe in you my soul, the other I am must not
> > abase itself to you,
> And you must not be abased to the other.

I think this means that Whitman has created his per-
sona of the rough Walt because only mutual abasement
ensues from any commerce between his real me, or inward
self, and his soul. Fascinating as an admission, this calls for
commentary, or at least creative surmise. *Leaves of Grass*
emerged only because the persona was achieved; until
then nothing could establish a dialogue, let alone a har-
mony, between Whitman's self and soul. His personality
and character could only lower themselves to one another.
The forging of a new personality, flamboyant and self-
reliant, provided not a mediation between soul and real

self (nothing, for Whitman, could do that) but allowed a love of equals between the rough Walt and his unknown soul. "Our father Walt Whitman," as James Wright called him in his splendid "Minneapolis Poem," became not the captain but the lover of his own soul. "Nothing is got for nothing," Emerson's restatement of the iron New England law of compensation, came into play with the rebellion against the vaunting Walt by the real me or me myself in the great *Sea-Drift* elegy for the self, "As I Ebb'd with the Ocean of Life":

> O baffled, balk'd, bent to the very earth,
> Oppress'd with myself that I have dared to open
>   my mouth,
> Aware now that amid all that blab whose echoes
>   recoil upon me I have not once had the least
>   idea who or what I am,
> But that before all my arrogant poems the real Me
>   stands yet untouch'd, untold, altogether
>   unreach'd,
> Withdrawn far, mocking me with mock-
>   congratulatory signs and bows,
> With peals of distant ironical laughter at every
>   word I have written,
> Pointing in silence to these songs, and then to the
>   sand beneath.

"The real Me" has its revenge, "Pointing in silence to these songs, and then to the sand beneath." The songs are there because Whitman is walking the beach, *Leaves of Grass* in his hands, fragments shored against his ruins. Hart Crane, superb interpreter of Whitman in Crane's own poems, catches this precisely in his "Passage":

> Touching an opening laurel, I found
> A thief beneath, my stolen book in hand.

The real Me, dusky demon and dark brother, steals the book back, but it was stolen from him in the first place. In *The Bridge*, Crane directs us to Whitman's central trope, the "tally":

> O, upward from the dead
> Thou bringest tally, and a pact, new bound
> Of living brotherhood!

To understand the "tally" and "tallying" is to be a long way forward in the reading of Whitman. The word "tally" is founded upon the Latin *talea*, a cutting or twig, clearly in Whitman's mind when he yields up his sprig of lilac to Lincoln's passing cortege. For Whitman, the "tally" has a range of meanings: to count up one's poems, to constitute a double or agreement, to notch one's score of autoerotic episodes upon a cutting. In England, and then in the American vernacular, an aura of illicit sexuality became attached to the word: a girl friend is a "tallywoman" and the male genitalia is "tallywags" or "tallywhacks" in parts of the United States until this day.

Section 25 of "Song of Myself" begins with Whitman at his strongest and most persuasive:

> Dazzling and tremendous how quick the sun-rise
>   would kill me,
> If I could not now and always send sun-rise out of
>   me.
>
> We also ascend dazzling and tremendous as the
>   sun,
> We found our own O my soul in the calm and cool
>   of the day-break.

Yahweh liked to walk in the Garden in the cool of the morning. Walt Whitman, for literary Americans, is a kind

of universal father, and at his most intense he amiably as-
serted his godhood. I cannot think of another poet who
could sustain the line: "If I could not now and always send
sun-rise out of me." This is most memorably reprised by
Wallace Stevens, involuntary disciple of the tramp poet:

> In the far South the sun of autumn is passing
> Like Walt Whitman walking along a ruddy shore.
> He is singing and chanting the things that are part
> of him,
> The worlds that were and will be, death and day.
> Nothing is final, he chants. No man shall see the
> end.
> His beard is of fire and his staff is a leaping flame.

No one, not Lorca nor Hart Crane nor Fernando Pes-
soa's Alvaro de Campos, has done so well by Whitman, or
would have pleased him so much, particularly by the anti-
apocalypticism of this superb celebration. Walt is an anti-
thetical sun-rise, *contra naturam*, and yet he is also natural-
all-too-natural, in the mode of Onan, tally-whacking-off:

> I underlying causes to balance them at last,
> My knowledge my live parts, it keeping tally with
> the meaning of all things.

Whitman keeps tally by autoerotic ecstasy; in one of
his late *Whispers of Heavenly Death* poems, he announces:
"All sorrow, labor, suffering, I, tallying it, absorb in my-
self." This carries an inward eros beyond anything we
easily comprehend. For Whitman, to tally is to think the old
thoughts of counterparts, not as duplicates yet not quite as
mere resemblances. When the penultimate section 15 of
the "Lilacs" elegy begins with: "To the tally of my soul," I
suggest that the poet is being very precise. The Song of
Death chanted by the hermit-thrush not only holds Whit-

man rapt by its charm, but also: "And the voice of my spirit tallied the song of the bird." Tallying is extended beyond its verbal limits: it is an esoteric Whitmanian term for the process by which at last he comes to know his own soul.

4

John Hollander says of Whitmanian troping: "His literal is elusively figurative." That wisdom makes me wonder at the autoerotic literalism of "Song of Myself" and "Spontaneous Me." To find the demarcations between literal and figurative in Whitman is an effort of which criticism so far is innocent. I turn to "The Sleepers" to begin such an effort.

In 1855, like every other poem in the first *Leaves of Grass*, this wonderfully strange vision was untitled. In 1856, it became "Night Poem"; in 1860, "Sleep-Chasings," and from 1871 on, "The Sleepers." But from 1881 on, Whitman unfortunately omitted two powerful passages. I have restored them in this volume by printing the text of the 1855 edition ("I wander all night in my vision"). The poet's belated anxiety about these two visions, after he had kept them public for more than a quarter century, warrants pondering. After what is now section 1, this was deleted:

> O hotcheeked and blushing! O foolish hectic!
> O for pity's sake, no one must see me now! . . . .
>   my clothes were stolen while I was abed,
> Now I am thrust forth, where shall I run?
>
> Pier that I saw dimly last night when I looked
>   from the windows,
> Pier out from the main, let me catch myself with
>   you and stay . . . . I will not chafe you;
> I feel ashamed to go naked about the world,
> And am curious to know where my feet stand . . . .
>   and what is this flooding me, childhood or

> manhood . . . . and the hunger that crosses
> the bridge between.
>
> The cloth laps a first sweet eating and drinking,
> Laps life-swelling yolks . . . . laps ear of rose-
>   corn, milky and just ripened:
> The white teeth stay, and the boss-tooth advances
>   in darkness,
> And liquor is spilled on lips and bosoms by touching
>   glasses, and the best liquor afterward.

I suspect that the "boss-tooth" or phallus and the spermatic "best liquor afterward" did not so much prompt the exile of these lines as did the image of the naked Whitman thrust forth upon the cosmos. By 1881, the Good Gray Poet had his dignity to maintain. The other vetoed passage, after section 6, is far more extraordinary:

> Now Lucifer was not dead . . . . or if he was I am
>   his sorrowful terrible heir;
> I have been wronged . . . . I am oppressed . . . .
>   I hate him that oppresses me,
> I will either destroy him, or he shall release me.
>
> Damn him! how he does defile me,
> How he informs against my brother and sister and
>   takes pay for their blood,
> How he laughs when I look down the bend after
>   the steamboat that carries away my woman.
>
> Now the vast dusk bulk that is the whale's bulk . . . .
>   it seems mine,
> Warily, sportsman! though I lie so sleepy and
>   sluggish, my tap is death.

The speaker would appear to be an African-American slave, identifying himself with the devil because his white oppressor is God. In a Lucifer to Leviathan metamorphosis, the slave becomes a black Moby Dick, whose "vast dusk bulk" properly menaces the presumably white sportsman. Prophetic and eloquent as this was, why did Whitman in 1881 suppress it? He seems to have touched one of his synecdochal limits, akin to his Quaker-influenced revulsion from identification with beggars in the transition between sections 37 and 38 of "Song of Myself."

"The Sleepers" is a hazardous poem, with Whitman always on the verge of losing his identity to night and the sea. The "beautiful gigantic swimmer" becomes the "brave corpse," and every other incarnation of the self in the poem seems in jeopardy. Of all the poems in the first *Leaves of Grass*, "The Sleepers" has the dark function of introducing Whitman's fourfold trope of the unknown soul: night, death, the mother, and the sea, with sleep their composite form. Though the poem concludes in an expression of trust in the sleeper's night, Whitman's overstates this confidence:

> Why should I be afraid to trust myself to you?
> I am not afraid . . . . I have been well brought
>   forward by you;
> I love the rich running day, but I do not desert her
>   in whom I lay so long;
> I know not how I came of you, and I know not
>   where I go with you . . . . but I know I came
>   well and shall go well.
>
> I will stop only a time with the night . . . . and
>   rise betimes.
>
> I will duly pass the day O my mother and duly
>   return to you;

The astonishing new poem in the second *Leaves of Grass* was, and remains, "Crossing Brooklyn Ferry," originally called "Sun-Down Poem." I am uncertain whether the "face to face" of the opening lines actually is a Biblical allusion. When Jacob said, at Penuel, that he had seen one of the Elohim "face to face" in an all-night wrestling match, he was expressing joy and wonder at his own survival. Whitman's "face to face" seems to me very different:

> Flood-tide below me! I see you face to face!
> Clouds of the west—sun there half an hour high—
>   I see you also face to face.

"Crossing Brooklyn Ferry" is not a crisis-poem. Rather, it is Whitman's major confrontation with his readers, reaffirming similar stances in the first *Leaves of Grass*, but in a finer tone, including the remarkable epiphany of section 6:

> It is not upon you alone the dark patches fall,
> The dark threw its patches down upon me also,
> The best I had done seem'd to me blank and
>   suspicious,
> My great thoughts as I supposed them, were they
>   not in reality meagre?
> Nor is it you alone who know what it is to be evil,
> I am he who knew what it was to be evil,
> I too knotted the old knot of contrariety,
> Blabb'd, blush'd, resented, lied, stole, grudg'd,
> Had guile, anger, lust, hot wishes I dared not speak,
> Was wayward, vain, greedy, shallow, sly, cowardly,
>   malignant,
> The wolf, the snake, the hog, not wanting in me,

The cheating look, the frivolous word, the
      adulterous wish, not wanting,
Refusals, hates, postponements, meanness,
      laziness, none of these wanting,
Was one with the rest, the days and haps of the rest,
Was call'd by my nighest name by clear loud
      voices of young men as they saw me
      approaching or passing,
Felt their arms on my neck as I stood, or the
      negligent leaning of their flesh against me
      as I sat,
Saw many I loved in the street or ferry-boat or
      public assembly, yet never told them a word,
Lived the same life with the rest, the same old
      laughing, gnawing, sleeping,
Play'd the part that still looks back on the actor or
      actress,
The same old role, the role that is what we make
      it, as great as we like,
Or as small as we like, or both great and small.

Edgar, disguised as Tom O'Bedlam in *King Lear*, tells
the mad king, out on the heath, of his own supposed past:
"False of heart, light of ear, bloody of hand; hog in sloth,
fox in stealth, wolf in greediness, dog in madness, lion in
prey" (Act III, scene iv, 92–93). Whitman echoes Edgar in:
"The wolf, the snake, the hog, not wanting in me," and
elsewhere in section 6. Was Whitman, on some level, im-
plying that his persona was a disguise like Edgar's Poor
Tom? Certainly Whitman is aware of role-playing "the
part that still looks back on the actor or actress."

    "Crossing Brooklyn Ferry" balances itself intricately
between flood-tide and ebb-tide, a balance that vanishes in
Whitman's three great elegies, "Out of the Cradle End-

lessly Rocking," "As I Ebb'd with the Ocean of Life," and "When Lilacs Last in the Dooryard Bloom'd."

The reader, considering the final passages of each of these, might ponder three tropes in particular out of many possibilities: "my dusky demon and brother"; "Just as much whence we come that blare of the cloud-trumpets"; "the tallying chant, the echo arous'd in my soul." The "dusky demon and brother" is the Real me or Me myself. Those cloud-trumpets, like Shelley's "trumpet of a prophecy," testify to the poet's battered yet authentic literary immortality. And "the tallying chant" is all of Whitman's strongest poetry, the central voice of American literature.

Harold Bloom
2002

I

**Early Notebook Fragments
of "Song of Myself"**

I am your voice—It was tied in you—In me it begins to
      talk.
I celebrate myself to celebrate every man and woman
      alive;
I loosen the tongue that was tied in them,
It begins to talk out of my mouth.

I celebrate myself to celebrate you:
I say the same word for every man and woman alive.
And I say that the soul is not greater than the body,
And I say that the body is not greater than the soul.

———

I am the poet of reality
I say the earth is not an echo
Nor man an apparition;
But that all the things seen are real,
The witness and albic dawn of things equally real
I have split the earth and the hard coal and rocks and
      the solid bed of the sea
And went down to reconnoitre there a long time,
And bring back a report,
And I understand that those are positive and dense
      every one
And that what they seem to the child they are
And the world is no joke,
Nor any part of it a sham

———

One touch of a tug of me has unhaltered all my senses
     but feeling
That pleases the rest so, they have given up to it in
     submission
They are all emulous to swap themselves off for what it
     can do to them.
Every one must be a touch
Or else she will abdicate and nibble only at the edges of
     feeling.

They move caressingly up and down my body
They leave themselves and come with bribes to
     whatever part of me touches.—
To my lips, to the palms of my hands, and whatever my
     hands hold.
Each brings the best she has,
For each is in love with touch.
I do not wonder that one feeling now does so much
     for me,
He is free of all the rest,—and swiftly begets offspring
     of them, better than the dams.
A touch now reads me a library of knowledge in an instant.
It smells for me the fragrance of wine and lemon-blows.
It tastes for me ripe strawberries and mellons,—
It talks for me with a tongue of its own,
It finds an ear wherever it rests or taps.
It brings the rest around it, and they all stand on a
     headland and mock me
They have left me to touch, and taken their place on a
     headland.

The sentries have deserted every other part of me
They have left me helpless to the torrent of touch
They have all come to the headland to witness and assist
	against me.—
I roam about drunk and stagger
I am given up by traitors,
I talk wildly I am surely out of my head,
I am myself the greatest traitor.
I went myself first to the headland

Unloose me, touch, you are taking the breath from my
	throat!
Unbar your gates you are too much for me
Fierce Wrestler! do you keep your heaviest grip for the
	last?
Will you sting me most even at parting?
Will you struggle even at the threshold with spasms
	more delicious than all before?
Does it make you to ache so to leave me?
Do you wish to show me that even what you did before
	was nothing to what you can do?
Or have you and all the rest combined to see how much
	I can endure?
Pass as you will; take drops of my life, if that is what you
	are after
Only pass to some one else, for I can contain you no
	longer
I held more than I thought
I did not think I was big enough for so much ecstasy
Or that a touch could take it all out of me.

———

Afar in the sky was a nest,
And my soul flew thither and squat, and looked out
And saw the journeywork of suns and systems of suns,
And that a leaf of grass is not less than they
And that the pismire is equally perfect, and all grains of
    sand, and every egg of the wren,
And the tree-toad is a chef' douvre for the highest,
And the running blackberry would adorn the parlors of
    Heaven
And the cow crunching with depressed neck surpasses
    every statue,
And pictures great and small crowd the rail-fence, and
    hang on its heaped stones and elder and poke-weed,
And a mouse is miracle enough to stagger trillions of
    infidels.
And I cannot put my toe anywhere to the ground,
But it must touch numberless and curious books
Each one scorning all that schools and science can do
    fully to translate them.
And the salt marsh and creek have delicious odor,
And potato and ear of maize make a fat breakfast,
And huckleberrys from the woods distill joyous
    deliriums.

The crowds naked in the bath,
Can your sight behold them as with oyster's eyes?
Do you take the attraction of gravity for nothing?
Does the negress bear no children?
Are they never handsome? Do they not thrive?
Will cabinet officers become blue or yellow from
      excessive gin?
Shall I receive the great things of the spirit on easier
      terms than I do a note of hand?
Who examines the philosophies in the market less than
      a basket of peaches or barrels of salt fish?
Who accepts chemistry on tradition?
The light picks out a bishop or pope no more than the
      rest.
A mouse is miracle enough to stagger billions of infidels.

In vain were nails driven through my hands.
I remember my crucifixion and bloody coronation
I remember the mockers and the buffeting insults
The sepulchre and the white linen have yielded me up
I am alive in New York and San Francisco,
Again I tread the streets after two thousand years.
Not all the traditions can put vitality in churches
They are not alive, they are cold mortar and brick,
I can easily build as good, and so can you:—
Books are not men—

7

———

There is no word in any tongue,
No array, no form of symbol,
To tell his infatuation
Who would define the scope and purpose of God.

Mostly this we have of God; we have man.
Lo, the Sun;
Its glory floods the moon,
Which of a night shines in some turbid pool,
Shaken by soughing winds;
And there are sparkles mad and tossed and broken,
And their archetype is the sun.

Of God I know not;
But this I know;
I can comprehend no being more wonderful than man;
Man, before the rage of whose passions the storms of
        Heaven are but a breath;
Before whose caprices the lightning is slow and less
        fatal;
Man, microcosm of all Creation's wildness, terror,
        beauty and power,
And whose folly and wickedness are in nothing else
        existent.
O dirt, you corpse, I reckon you are good manure—but
        that I do not smell—
I smell your beautiful white roses—
I kiss your leafy lips—I slide my hands for the brown
        melons of your breasts.

II

Song of Myself

1

I celebrate myself, and sing myself,
And what I assume you shall assume,
For every atom belonging to me as good belongs to you.

I loafe and invite my soul,
I lean and loafe at my ease observing a spear of summer
    grass.

My tongue, every atom of my blood, form'd from this
    soil, this air,
Born here of parents born here from parents the same,
    and their parents the same,
I, now thirty-seven years old in perfect health begin,
Hoping to cease not till death.

Creeds and schools in abeyance,
Retiring back a while sufficed at what they are, but
    never forgotten,
I harbor for good or bad, I permit to speak at every
    hazard,
Nature without check with original energy.

2

Houses and rooms are full of perfumes, the shelves are
    crowded with perfumes,
I breathe the fragrance myself and know it and like it,
The distillation would intoxicate me also, but I shall not
    let it.

The atmosphere is not a perfume, it has no taste of the
       distillation, it is odorless,
It is for my mouth forever, I am in love with it,
I will go to the bank by the wood and become
       undisguised and naked,
I am mad for it to be in contact with me.

The smoke of my own breath,
Echoes, ripples, buzz'd whispers, love-root, silk-thread,
       crotch and vine,
My respiration and inspiration, the beating of my heart,
       the passing of blood and air through my lungs,
The sniff of green leaves and dry leaves, and of the
       shore and dark-color'd sea-rocks, and of hay in
       the barn,
The sound of the belch'd words of my voice loos'd to
       the eddies of the wind,
A few light kisses, a few embraces, a reaching around
       of arms,
The play of shine and shade on the trees as the supple
       boughs wag,
The delight alone or in the rush of the streets, or along
       the fields and hill-sides,
The feeling of health, the full-noon trill, the song of me
       rising from bed and meeting the sun.

Have you reckon'd a thousand acres much? have you
       reckon'd the earth much?
Have you practis'd so long to learn to read?
Have you felt so proud to get at the meaning of poems?

Stop this day and night with me and you shall possess
    the origin of all poems,
You shall possess the good of the earth and sun, (there
    are millions of suns left,)
You shall no longer take things at second or third hand,
    nor look through the eyes of the dead, nor feed on
    the spectres in books,
You shall not look through my eyes either, nor take
    things from me,
You shall listen to all sides and filter them from your self.

3

I have heard what the talkers were talking, the talk of
    the beginning and the end,
But I do not talk of the beginning or the end.

There was never any more inception than there is now,
Nor any more youth or age than there is now,
And will never be any more perfection than there is now,
Nor any more heaven or hell than there is now.

Urge and urge and urge,
Always the procreant urge of the world.

Out of the dimness opposite equals advance, always
    substance and increase, always sex,
Always a knit of identity, always distinction, always a
    breed of life.

To elaborate is no avail, learn'd and unlearn'd feel that it
   is so.

Sure as the most certain sure, plumb in the uprights,
   well entretied, braced in the beams,
Stout as a horse, affectionate, haughty, electrical,
I and this mystery here we stand.

Clear and sweet is my soul, and clear and sweet is all
   that is not my soul.

Lack one lacks both, and the unseen is proved by the seen,
Till that becomes unseen and receives proof in its turn.

Showing the best and dividing it from the worst age
   vexes age,
Knowing the perfect fitness and equanimity of things,
   while they discuss I am silent, and go bathe and
   admire myself.

Welcome is every organ and attribute of me, and of any
   man hearty and clean,
Not an inch nor a particle of an inch is vile, and none
   shall be less familiar than the rest.

I am satisfied—I see, dance, laugh, sing;
As the hugging and loving bed-fellow sleeps at my side
   through the night, and withdraws at the peep of the
   day with stealthy tread,
Leaving me baskets cover'd with white towels swelling
   the house with their plenty,
Shall I postpone my acceptation and realization and
   scream at my eyes,
That they turn from gazing after and down the road,

And forthwith cipher and show me to a cent,
Exactly the value of one and exactly the value of two,
    and which is ahead?

4

Trippers and askers surround me,
People I meet, the effect upon me of my early life or the
    ward and city I live in, or the nation,
The latest dates, discoveries, inventions, societies,
    authors old and new,
My dinner, dress, associates, looks, compliments, dues,
The real or fancied indifference of some man or woman
    I love,
The sickness of one of my folks or of myself, or ill-doing
    or loss or lack of money, or depressions or
    exaltations,
Battles, the horrors of fratricidal war, the fever of
    doubtful news, the fitful events;
These come to me days and nights and go from me again,
But they are not the Me myself.

Apart from the pulling and hauling stands what I am,
Stands amused, complacent, compassionating, idle,
    unitary,
Looks down, is erect, or bends an arm on an impalpable
    certain rest,
Looking with side-curved head curious what will
    come next,
Both in and out of the game and watching and wondering
    at it.

Backward I see in my own days where I sweated through
  fog with linguists and contenders,
I have no mockings or arguments, I witness and wait.

5

I believe in you my soul, the other I am must not abase
  itself to you,
And you must not be abased to the other.

Loafe with me on the grass, loose the stop from your
  throat,
Not words, not music or rhyme I want, not custom or
  lecture, not even the best,
Only the lull I like, the hum of your valvèd voice.

I mind how once we lay such a transparent summer
  morning,
How you settled your head athwart my hips and gently
  turn'd over upon me,
And parted the shirt from my bosom-bone, and plunged
  your tongue to my bare-stript heart,
And reach'd till you felt my beard, and reach'd till you
  held my feet.

Swiftly arose and spread around me the peace and
  knowledge that pass all the argument of the earth,
And I know that the hand of God is the promise of
  my own,
And I know that the spirit of God is the brother of
  my own,
And that all the men ever born are also my brothers,
  and the women my sisters and lovers,

And that a kelson of the creation is love,
And limitless are leaves stiff or drooping in the fields,
And brown ants in the little wells beneath them,
And mossy scabs of the worm fence, heap'd stones,
     elder, mullein and poke-weed.

6

A child said *What is the grass?* fetching it to me with full
     hands;
How could I answer the child? I do not know what it is
     any more than he.
I guess it must be the flag of my disposition, out of
     hopeful green stuff woven.

Or I guess it is the handkerchief of the Lord,
A scented gift and remembrancer designedly dropt,
Bearing the owner's name someway in the corners, that
     we may see and remark, and say *Whose?*

Or I guess the grass is itself a child, the produced babe
     of the vegetation.

Or I guess it is a uniform hieroglyphic,
And it means, Sprouting alike in broad zones and
     narrow zones,
Growing among black folks as among white,
Kanuck, Tuckahoe, Congressman, Cuff, I give them the
     same, I receive them the same.

And now it seems to me the beautiful uncut hair of
     graves.

Tenderly will I use you curling grass,
It may be you transpire from the breasts of young men,
It may be if I had known them I would have loved them,
It may be you are from old people, or from offspring
    taken soon out of their mothers' laps,
And here you are the mothers' laps.

This grass is very dark to be from the white heads of old
    mothers,
Darker than the colorless beards of old men,
Dark to come from under the faint red roofs of mouths.

O I perceive after all so many uttering tongues,
And I perceive they do not come from the roofs of
    mouths for nothing.

I wish I could translate the hints about the dead young
    men and women,
And the hints about old men and mothers, and the
    offspring taken soon out of their laps.

What do you think has become of the young and
    old men?
And what do you think has become of the women and
    children?

They are alive and well somewhere,
The smallest sprout shows there is really no death,
And if ever there was it led forward life, and does not
    wait at the end to arrest it,
And ceas'd the moment life appear'd.

All goes onward and outward, nothing collapses,
And to die is different from what any one supposed,
     and luckier.

7

Has any one supposed it lucky to be born?
I hasten to inform him or her it is just as lucky to die,
     and I know it.

I pass death with the dying and birth with the new-
     wash'd babe, and am not contain'd between my hat
     and boots,
And peruse manifold objects, no two alike and every one
     good,
The earth good and the stars good, and their adjuncts
     all good.

I am not an earth nor an adjunct of an earth,
I am the mate and companion of people, all just as
     immortal and fathomless as myself,
(They do not know how immortal, but I know.)

Every kind for itself and its own, for me mine male and
     female,
For me those that have been boys and that love women,
For me the man that is proud and feels how it stings to
     be slighted,
For me the sweet-heart and the old maid, for me
     mothers and the mothers of mothers,
For me lips that have smiled, eyes that have shed tears,
For me children and the begetters of children.

Undrape! you are not guilty to me, nor stale nor
    discarded,
I see through the broadcloth and gingham whether or no,
And am around, tenacious, acquisitive, tireless, and
    cannot be shaken away.

8

The little one sleeps in its cradle,
I lift the gauze and look a long time, and silently brush
    away flies with my hand.

The youngster and the red-faced girl turn aside up the
    bushy hill,
I peeringly view them from the top.

The suicide sprawls on the bloody floor of the bedroom,
I witness the corpse with its dabbled hair, I note where
    the pistol has fallen.

The blab of the pave, tires of carts, sluff of boot-soles,
    talk of the promenaders,
The heavy omnibus, the driver with his interrogating
    thumb, the clank of the shod horses on the granite
    floor,
The snow-sleighs, clinking, shouted jokes, pelts of
    snow-balls,
The hurrahs for popular favorites, the fury of
    rous'd mobs,
The flap of the curtain'd litter, a sick man inside borne
    to the hospital,

The meeting of enemies, the sudden oath, the blows
     and fall,
The excited crowd, the policeman with his star quickly
     working his passage to the centre of the crowd,
The impassive stones that receive and return so many
     echoes,
What groans of over-fed or half-starv'd who fall
     sunstruck or in fits,
What exclamations of women taken suddenly who hurry
     home and give birth to babes,
What living and buried speech is always vibrating here,
     what howls restrain'd by decorum,
Arrests of criminals, slights, adulterous offers made,
     acceptances, rejections with convex lips,
I mind them or the show or resonance of them—I come
     and I depart.

9

The big doors of the country barn stand open and ready,
The dried grass of the harvest-time loads the
     slow-drawn wagon,
The clear light plays on the brown gray and green
     intertinged,
The armfuls are pack'd to the sagging mow.

I am there, I help, I came stretch'd atop of the load,
I felt its soft jolts, one leg reclined on the other,
I jump from the cross-beams and seize the clover and
     timothy,
And roll head over heels and tangle my hair full of wisps.

10

Alone far in the wilds and mountains I hunt,
Wandering amazed at my own lightness and glee,
In the late afternoon choosing a safe spot to pass the
night,
Kindling a fire and broiling the fresh-kill'd game,
Falling asleep on the gather'd leaves with my dog and
gun by my side.

The Yankee clipper is under her sky-sails, she cuts the
sparkle and scud,
My eyes settle the land, I bend at her prow or shout
joyously from the deck.

The boatmen and clam-diggers arose early and stopt
for me,
I tuck'd my trowser-ends in my boots and went and had
a good time;
You should have been with us that day round the
chowder-kettle.

I saw the marriage of the trapper in the open air in the
far west, the bride was a red girl,
Her father and his friends sat near cross-legged and
dumbly smoking, they had moccasins to their feet and
large thick blankets hanging from their shoulders,
On a bank lounged the trapper, he was drest mostly in
skins, his luxuriant beard and curls protected his
neck, he held his bride by the hand,
She had long eyelashes, her head was bare, her coarse
straight locks descended upon her voluptuous limbs
and reach'd to her feet.

The runaway slave came to my house and stopt outside,
I heard his motions crackling the twigs of the
    woodpile,
Through the swung half-door of the kitchen I saw him
    limpsy and weak,
And went where he sat on a log and led him in and
    assured him,
And brought water and fill'd a tub for his sweated body
    and bruis'd feet,
And gave him a room that enter'd from my own, and
    gave him some coarse clean clothes,
And remember perfectly well his revolving eyes and his
    awkwardness,
And remember putting plasters on the galls of his neck
    and ankles;
He staid with me a week before he was recuperated and
    pass'd north,
I had him sit next me at table, my fire-lock lean'd in the
    corner.

11

Twenty-eight young men bathe by the shore,
Twenty-eight young men and all so friendly;
Twenty-eight years of womanly life and all so lonesome.

She owns the fine house by the rise of the bank,
She hides handsome and richly drest aft the blinds of
    the window.

Which of the young men does she like the best?
Ah the homeliest of them is beautiful to her.

Where are you off to, lady? for I see you,
You splash in the water there, yet stay stock still in your
　　room.

Dancing and laughing along the beach came the
　　　twenty-ninth bather,
The rest did not see her, but she saw them and loved
　　them.

The beards of the young men glisten'd with wet, it ran
　　　from their long hair,
Little streams pass'd all over their bodies.

An unseen hand also pass'd over their bodies,
It descended tremblingly from their temples and ribs.

The young men float on their backs, their white bellies
　　　bulge to the sun, they do not ask who seizes fast
　　　to them,
They do not know who puffs and declines with pendant
　　　and bending arch,
They do not think whom they souse with spray.

12

The butcher-boy puts off his killing-clothes, or sharpens
　　　his knife at the stall in the market,
I loiter enjoying his repartee and his shuffle and
　　break-down.

Blacksmiths with grimed and hairy chests environ
　　　the anvil,
Each has his main-sledge, they are all out, there is a
　　great heat in the fire.

From the cinder-strew'd threshold I follow their
     movements,
The lithe sheer of their waists plays even with their
     massive arms,
Overhand the hammers swing, overhand so slow,
     overhand so sure,
They do not hasten, each man hits in his place.

13

The negro holds firmly the reins of his four horses, the
     block swags underneath on its tied-over chain,
The negro that drives the long dray of the stone-yard,
     steady and tall he stands pois'd on one leg on the
     string-piece,
His blue shirt exposes his ample neck and breast and
     loosens over his hip-band,
His glance is calm and commanding, he tosses the
     slouch of his hat away from his forehead,
The sun falls on his crispy hair and mustache, falls on
     the black of his polish'd and perfect limbs.

I behold the picturesque giant and love him, and I do
     not stop there,
I go with the team also.

In me the caresser of life wherever moving, backward as
     well as forward sluing,
To niches aside and junior bending, not a person or
     object missing,
Absorbing all to myself and for this song.

Oxen that rattle the yoke and chain or halt in the leafy
    shade, what is that you express in your eyes?
It seems to me more than all the print I have read in
    my life.

My tread scares the wood-drake and wood-duck on my
    distant and day-long ramble,
They rise together, they slowly circle around.

I believe in those wing'd purposes,
And acknowledge red, yellow, white, playing within me,
And consider green and violet and the tufted crown
    intentional,
And do not call the tortoise unworthy because she is not
    something else,
And the jay in the woods never studied the gamut, yet
    trills pretty well to me,
And the look of the bay mare shames silliness out of me.

14

The wild gander leads his flock through the cool night,
Ya-honk he says, and sounds it down to me like an
    invitation,
The pert may suppose it meaningless, but I listening
    close,
Find its purpose and place up there toward the wintry sky.

The sharp-hoof'd moose of the north, the cat on the
    house-sill, the chickadee, the prairie-dog,
The litter of the grunting sow as they tug at her teats,

The brood of the turkey-hen and she with her
        half-spread wings,
I see in them and myself the same old law.

The press of my foot to the earth springs a hundred
        affections,
They scorn the best I can do to relate them.

I am enamour'd of growing out-doors,
Of men that live among cattle or taste of the ocean
        or woods,
Of the builders and steerers of ships and the wielders of
        axes and mauls, and the drivers of horses,
I can eat and sleep with them week in and week out.

What is commonest, cheapest, nearest, easiest, is Me,
Me going in for my chances, spending for vast returns,
Adorning myself to bestow myself on the first that will
        take me,
Not asking the sky to come down to my good will,
Scattering it freely forever.

15

The pure contralto sings in the organ loft,
The carpenter dresses his plank, the tongue of his
        foreplane whistles its wild ascending lisp,
The married and unmarried children ride home to their
        Thanksgiving dinner,
The pilot seizes the king-pin, he heaves down with a
        strong arm,

The mate stands braced in the whale-boat, lance and
     harpoon are ready,
The duck-shooter walks by silent and cautious stretches,
The deacons are ordain'd with cross'd hands at the alter,
The spinning-girl retreats and advances to the hum of
     the big wheel,
The farmer stops by the bars as he walks on a First-day
     loafe and looks at the oats and rye,
The lunatic is carried at last to the asylum a confirm'd
     case,
(He will never sleep any more as he did in the cot in his
     mother's bed-room;)
The jour printer with gray head and gaunt jaws works at
     his case,
He turns his quid of tobacco while his eyes blurr with
     the manuscript;
The malform'd limbs are tied to the surgeon's table,
What is removed drops horribly in a pail;
The quadroon girl is sold at the auction-stand, the
     drunkard nods by the bar-room stove,
The machinist rolls up his sleeves, the policeman travels
     his beat, the gate-keeper marks who pass,
The young fellow drives the express-wagon, (I love him,
     though I do not know him;)
The half-breed straps on his light boots to compete in
     the race,
The western turkey-shooting draws old and young,
     some lean on their rifles, some sit on logs,
Out from the crowd steps the marksman, takes his
     position, levels his piece;
The groups of newly-come immigrants cover the wharf
     or levee,

As the woolly-pates hoe in the sugar-field, the overseer
	views them from his saddle,
The bugle calls in the ball-room, the gentlemen run for
	their partners, the dancers bow to each other,
The youth lies awake in the cedar-roof'd garret and
	harks to the musical rain,
The Wolverine sets traps on the creek that helps fill the
	Huron,
The squaw wrapt in her yellow-hemm'd cloth is offering
	moccasins and bead-bags for sale,
The connoisseur peers along the exhibition-gallery with
	half-shut eyes bent sideways,
As the deck-hands make fast the steamboat the plank is
	thrown for the shore-going passengers,
The young sister holds out the skein while the elder
	sister winds it off in a ball, and stops now and then
	for the knots,
The one-year wife is recovering and happy having a
	week ago borne her first child,
The clean-hair'd Yankee girl works with her sewing-
	machine or in the factory or mill,
The paving-man leans on his two-handed rammer, the
	reporter's lead flies swiftly over the note-book, the
	sign-painter is lettering with blue and gold,
The canal boy trots on the tow-path, the book-keeper
	counts at his desk, the shoemaker waxes his thread,
The conductor beats time for the band and all the
	performers follow him,
The child is baptized, the convert is making his first
	professions,
The regatta is spread on the bay, the race is begun, (how
	the white sails sparkle!)

The drover watching his drove sings out to them that
would stray,
The pedler sweats with his pack on his back, (the
purchaser higgling about the odd cent;)
The bride unrumples her white dress, the minute-hand
of the clock moves slowly,
The opium-eater reclines with rigid head and just-
open'd lips,
The prostitute draggles her shawl, her bonnet bobs on
her tipsy and pimpled neck,
The crowd laugh at her blackguard oaths, the men jeer
and wink to each other,
(Miserable! I do not laugh at your oaths nor jeer you;)
The President holding a cabinet council is surrounded
by the great Secretaries,
On the piazza walk three matrons stately and friendly
with twined arms,
The crew of the fish-smack pack repeated layers of
halibut in the hold,
The Missourian crosses the plains toting his wares and
his cattle,
As the fare-collector goes through the train he gives
notice by the jingling of loose change,
The floor-men are laying the floor, the tinners are
tinning the roof, the masons are calling for mortar,
In single file each shouldering his hod pass onward the
laborers;
Seasons pursuing each other the indescribable crowd is
gather'd, it is the fourth of Seventh-month, (what
salutes of cannon and small arms!)

Seasons pursuing each other the plougher ploughs, the
      mower mows, and the winter-grain falls in the
      ground;
Off on the lakes the pike-fisher watches and waits by the
      hole in the frozen surface,
The stumps stand thick round the clearing, the squatter
      strikes deep with his axe,
Flatboatmen make fast towards dusk near the cotton-
      wood or pecan-trees,
Coon-seekers go through the regions of the Red river
      or through those drain'd by the Tennessee, or
      through those of the Arkansas,
Torches shine in the dark that hangs on the
      Chattahooche or Altamahaw,
Patriarchs sit at supper with sons and grandsons and
      great-grandsons around them,
In walls of adobie, in canvas tents, rest hunters and
      trappers after their day's sport,
The city sleeps and the country sleeps,
The living sleep for their time, the dead sleep for
      their time,
The old husband sleeps by his wife and the young
      husband sleeps by his wife;
And these tend inward to me, and I tend outward
      to them,
And such as it is to be of these more or less I am,
And of these one and all I weave the song of myself.

I am of old and young, of the foolish as much as
the wise,

Regardless of others, ever regardful of others,

Maternal as well as paternal, a child as well as a man,

Stuff'd with the stuff that is coarse and stuff'd with the
stuff that is fine,

One of the Nation of many nations, the smallest the
same and the largest the same,

A Southerner soon as a Northerner, a planter nonchalant
and hospitable down by the Oconee I live,

A Yankee bound my own way ready for trade, my joints
the limberest joints on earth and the sternest joints
on earth,

A Kentuckian walking the vale of the Elkhorn in my
deer-skin leggings, a Louisianian or Georgian,

A boatman over lakes or bays or along coasts, a Hoosier,
Badger, Buckeye;

At home on Kanadian snow-shoes or up in the bush, or
with fishermen off Newfoundland,

At home in the fleet of ice-boats, sailing with the rest
and tacking,

At home on the hills of Vermont or in the woods of
Maine, or the Texan ranch,

Comrade of Californians, comrade of free North-
Westerners, (loving their big proportions,)

Comrade of raftsmen and coalmen, comrade of all who
shake hands and welcome to drink and meat,

A learner with the simplest, a teacher of the
thoughtfullest,

A novice beginning yet experient of myriads of seasons,
Of every hue and caste am I, of every rank and religion,
A farmer, mechanic, artist, gentleman, sailor, quaker,
Prisoner, fancy-man, rowdy, lawyer, physician, priest.

I resist any thing better than my own diversity,
Breathe the air but leave plenty after me,
And am not stuck up, and am in my place.

(The moth and the fish-eggs are in their place,
The bright suns I see and the dark suns I cannot see are
    in their place,
The palpable is in its place and the impalpable is in its
    place.)

17

These are really the thoughts of all men in all ages and
    lands, they are not original with me,
If they are not yours as much as mine they are nothing,
    or next to nothing,
If they are not the riddle and the untying of the riddle
    they are nothing,
If they are not just as close as they are distant they are
    nothing.

This is the grass that grows wherever the land is and the
    water is,
This the common air that bathes the globe.

With music strong I come, with my cornets and my
      drums,
I play not marches for accepted victors only, I play
      marches for conquer'd and slain persons.

Have you heard that it was good to gain the day?
I also say it is good to fall, battles are lost in the same
      spirit in which they are won.

I beat and pound for the dead,
I blow through my embouchures my loudest and gayest
      for them.

Vivas to those who have fail'd!
And to those whose war-vessels sank in the sea!
And to those themselves who sank in the sea!
And to all generals that lost engagements, and all
      overcome heroes!
And the numberless unknown heroes equal to the
      greatest heroes known!

19

This is the meal equally set, this the meat for natural
      hunger,
It is for the wicked just the same as the righteous,
      I make appointments with all,
I will not have a single person slighted or left away,
The kept-woman, sponger, thief, are hereby invited,
The heavy-lipp'd slave is invited, the venerealee is invited;
There shall be no difference between them and the rest.

This is the press of a bashful hand, this the float and
    odor of hair,
This the touch of my lips to yours, this the murmur of
    yearning,
This the far-off depth and height reflecting my own face,
This the thoughtful merge of myself, and the outlet again.

Do you guess I have some intricate purpose?
Well I have, for the Fourth-month showers have, and
    the mica on the side of a rock has.

Do you take it I would astonish?
Does the daylight astonish? does the early redstart
    twittering through the woods?
Do I astonish more than they?

This hour I tell things in confidence,
I might not tell everybody, but I will tell you.

20

Who goes there? hankering, gross, mystical, nude;
How is it I extract strength from the beef I eat?

What is a man anyhow? what am I? what are you?

All I mark as my own you shall offset it with your own,
Else it were time lost listening to me.

I do not snivel that snivel the world over,
That months are vacuums and the ground but wallow
    and filth.

Whimpering and truckling fold with powders for
    invalids, conformity goes to the fourth-remov'd,
I wear my hat as I please indoors or out.

Why should I pray? why should I venerate and be
    ceremonious?

Having pried through the strata, analyzed to a hair,
    counsel'd with doctors and calculated close,
I find no sweeter fat than sticks to my own bones.

In all people I see myself, none more and not one a
    barley-corn less,
And the good or bad I say of myself I say of them.

I know I am solid and sound,
To me the converging objects of the universe
    perpetually flow,
All are written to me, and I must get what the writing
    means.

I know I am deathless,
I know this orbit of mine cannot be swept by a
    carpenter's compass,
I know I shall not pass like a child's carlacue cut with a
    burnt stick at night.

I know I am august,
I do not trouble my spirit to vindicate itself or be
    understood,
I see that the elementary laws never apologize,
(I reckon I behave no prouder than the level I plant my
    house by, after all.)

I exist as I am, that is enough,
If no other in the world be aware I sit content,
And if each and all be aware I sit content.

One world is aware and by far the largest to me, and
  that is myself,
And whether I come to my own to-day or in ten
  thousand or ten million years,
I can cheerfully take it now, or with equal cheerfulness
  I can wait.

My foothold is tenon'd and mortis'd in granite,
I laugh at what you call dissolution,
And I know the amplitude of time.

21

I am the poet of the Body and I am the poet of the Soul,
The pleasures of heaven are with me and the pains of
  hell are with me,
The first I graft and increase upon myself, the latter
  I translate into a new tongue.

I am the poet of the woman the same as the man,
And I say it is as great to be a woman as to be a man,
And I say there is nothing greater than the mother
  of men.

I chant the chant of dilation or pride,
We have had ducking and deprecating about enough,
I show that size is only development.

Have you outstript the rest? are you the President?
It is a trifle, they will more than arrive there every one,
    and still pass on.

I am he that walks with the tender and growing night,
I call to the earth and sea half-held by the night.

Press close bare-bosom'd night—press close magnetic
    nourishing night!
Night of south winds—night of the large few stars!
Still nodding night—mad naked summer night.

Smile O voluptuous cool-breath'd earth!
Earth of the slumbering and liquid trees!
Earth of departed sunset—earth of the mountains
    misty-topt!
Earth of the vitreous pour of the full moon just tinged
    with blue!
Earth of shine and dark mottling the tide of the river!
Earth of the limpid gray of clouds brighter and clearer
    for my sake!
Far-swooping elbow'd earth—rich apple-blossom'd
    earth!
Smile, for your lover comes.

Prodigal, you have given me love—therefore I to you
    give love!
O unspeakable passionate love.

22

You sea! I resign myself to you also—I guess what
    you mean,
I behold from the beach your crooked inviting fingers,
I believe you refuse to go back without feeling of me,
We must have a turn together, I undress, hurry me out
    of sight of the land,
Cushion me soft, rock me in billowy drowse,
Dash me with amorous wet, I can repay you.

Sea of stretch'd ground-swells,
Sea breathing broad and convulsive breaths,
Sea of the brine of life and of unshovell'd yet always-
    ready graves,
Howler and scooper of storms, capricious and
    dainty sea,
I am integral with you, I too am of one phase and of all
    phases.

Partaker of influx and efflux I, extoller of hate and
    conciliation,
Extoller of amies and those that sleep in each others'
    arms.

I am he attesting sympathy,
(Shall I make my list of things in the house and skip the
    house that supports them?)

I am not the poet of goodness only, I do not decline to
    be the poet of wickedness also.

What blurt is this about virtue and about vice?
Evil propels me and reform of evil propels me, I stand
    indifferent,
My gait is no fault-finder's or rejecter's gait,
I moisten the roots of all that has grown.

Did you fear some scrofula out of the unflagging
    pregnancy?
Did you guess the celestial laws are yet to be work'd
    over and rectified?

I find one side a balance and the antipodal side a balance,
Soft doctrine as steady help as stable doctrine,
Thoughts and deeds of the present our rouse and
    early start.

This minute that comes to me over the past decillions,
There is no better than it and now.

What behaved well in the past or behaves well to-day is
    not such a wonder,
The wonder is always and always how there can be a
    mean man or an infidel.

23

Endless unfolding of words of ages!
And mine a word of the modern, the word En-Masse.

A word of the faith that never balks,
Here or henceforward it is all the same to me, I accept
    Time absolutely.

It alone is without flaw, it alone rounds and
    completes all,
That mystic baffling wonder alone completes all.

I accept Reality and dare not question it,
Materialism first and last imbuing.

Hurrah for positive science! long live exact
    demonstration!
Fetch stonecrop mixt with cedar and branches of lilac,
This is the lexicographer, this the chemist, this made a
    grammar of the old cartouches,
These mariners put the ship through dangerous
    unknown seas.
This is the geologist, this works with the scalpel, and
    this is a mathematician.

Gentlemen, to you the first honors always!
Your facts are useful, and yet they are not my dwelling,
I but enter by them to an area of my dwelling.

Less the reminders of properties told my words,
And more the reminders they of life untold, and of
    freedom and extrication,
And make short account of neuters and geldings, and
    favor men and women fully equipt,
And beat the gong of revolt, and stop with fugitives and
    them that plot and conspire.

24

Walt Whitman, a kosmos, of Manhattan the son,
Turbulent, fleshy, sensual, eating, drinking and breeding,
No sentimentalist, no stander above men and women or
    apart from them,
No more modest than immodest.

Unscrew the locks from the doors!
Unscrew the doors themselves from their jambs!

Whoever degrades another degrades me,
And whatever is done or said returns at last to me.

Through me the afflatus surging and surging, through
    me the current and index.

I speak the pass-word primeval, I give the sign of
    democracy,
By God! I will accept nothing which all cannot have
    their counterpart of on the same terms.

Through me many long dumb voices,
Voices of the interminable generations of prisoners
    and slaves,
Voices of the diseas'd and despairing and of thieves and
    dwarfs,
Voices of cycles of preparation and accretion,
And of the threads that connect the stars, and of wombs
    and of the father-stuff,
And of the rights of them the others are down upon,
Of the deform'd, trivial, flat, foolish, despised,
Fog in the air, beetles rolling balls of dung.

Through me forbidden voices,
Voices of sexes and lusts, voices veil'd and I remove
    the veil,
Voices indecent by me clarified and transfigur'd.

I do not press my fingers across my mouth,
I keep as delicate around the bowels as around the head
    and heart,
Copulation is no more rank to me than death is.

I believe in the flesh and the appetites,
Seeing, hearing, feeling, are miracles, and each part and
    tag of me is a miracle.

Divine am I inside and out, and I make holy whatever
    I touch or am touch'd from,
The scent of these arm-pits aroma finer than prayer,
This head more than churches, bibles, and all the creeds.

If I worship one thing more than another it shall be the
    spread of my own body, or any part of it,
Translucent mould of me it shall be you!
Shaded ledges and rests it shall be you!
Firm masculine colter it shall be you!
Whatever goes to the tilth of me it shall be you!
You my rich blood! your milky stream pale strippings
    of my life!
Breast that presses against other breasts it shall be you!
My brain it shall be your occult convolutions!
Root of wash'd sweet-flag! timorous pond-snipe! nest of
    guarded duplicate eggs! it shall be you!
Mix'd tussled hay of head, beard, brawn, it shall be you!

Trickling sap of maple, fibre of manly wheat, it shall
      be you!
Sun so generous it shall be you!
Vapors lighting and shading my face it shall be you!
You sweaty brooks and dews it shall be you!
Winds whose soft-tickling genitals rub against me it
      shall be you!
Broad muscular fields, branches of live oak, loving
      lounger in my winding paths, it shall be you!
Hands I have taken, face I have kiss'd, mortal I have
      ever touch'd, it shall be you.

I dote on myself, there is that lot of me and all so luscious,
Each moment and whatever happens thrills me with joy,
I cannot tell how my ankles bend, nor whence the cause
      of my faintest wish,
Nor the cause of the friendship I emit, nor the cause of
      the friendship I take again.

That I walk up my stoop, I pause to consider if it
      really be,
A morning-glory at my window satisfies me more than
      the metaphysics of books.

To behold the day-break!
The little light fades the immense and diaphanous
      shadows,
The air tastes good to my palate.

Hefts of the moving world at innocent gambols silently
      rising freshly exuding,
Scooting obliquely high and low.

Something I cannot see puts upward libidinous prongs,
Seas of bright juice suffuse heaven.

The earth by the sky staid with, the daily close of their
     junction,
The heav'd challenge from the east that moment over
     my head,
The mocking taunt. See then whether you shall be
     master!

25

Dazzling and tremendous how quick the sun-rise would
     kill me,
If I could not now and always send sun-rise out of me.

We also ascend dazzling and tremendous as the sun,
We found our own O my soul in the calm and cool of
     the day-break.

My voice goes after what my eyes cannot reach,
With the twirl of my tongue I encompass worlds and
     volumes of worlds.

Speech is the twin of my vision, it is unequal to measure
     itself,
It provokes me forever, it says sarcastically,
Walt you contain enough, why don't you let it out then?

Come now I will not be tantalized, you conceive too
     much of articulation,
Do you not know O speech how the buds beneath you
     are folded?

Waiting in gloom, protected by frost,
The dirt receding before my prophetical screams,
I underlying causes to balance them at last,
My knowledge my live parts, it keeping tally with the
    meaning of all things,
Happiness, (which whoever hears me let him or her set
    out in search of this day.)

My final merit I refuse you, I refuse putting from me
    what I really am,
Encompass worlds, but never try to encompass me,
I crowd your sleekest and best by simply looking
    toward you.

Writing and talk do not prove me,
I carry the plenum of proof and every thing else in my
    face,
With the hush of my lips I wholly confound the
    skeptic.

26

Now I will do nothing but listen,
To accrue what I hear into this song, to let sounds
    contribute toward it.

I hear bravuras of birds, bustle of growing wheat, gossip
    of flames, clack of sticks cooking my meals,
I hear the sound I love, the sound of the human voice,
I hear all sounds running together, combined, fused or
    following,

Sounds of the city and sounds out of the city, sounds of
     the day and night,
Talkative young ones to those that like them, the loud
     laugh of work-people at their meals,
The angry base of disjointed friendship, the faint tones
     of the sick,
The judge with hands tight to the desk, his pallid lips
     pronouncing a death-sentence,
The heave'e'yo of stevedores unlading ships by the
     wharves, the refrain of the anchor-lifters,
The ring of alarm-bells, the cry of fire, the whirr of
     swift-streaking engines and hose-carts with
     premonitory tinkles and color'd lights,
The steam-whistle, the solid roll of the train of
     approaching cars,
The slow march play'd at the head of the association
     marching two and two,
(They go to guard some corpse, the flag-tops are draped
     with black muslin.)

I hear the violoncello, ('tis the young man's heart's
     complaint,)
I hear the key'd cornet, it glides quickly in through
     my ears,
It shakes mad-sweet pangs through my belly and
     breast.

I hear the chorus, it is a grand opera,
Ah this indeed is music—this suits me.

A tenor large and fresh as the creation fills me,
The orbic flex of his mouth is pouring and filling me full.

I hear the train'd soprano (what work with hers is this?)
The orchestra whirls me wider than Uranus flies,
It wrenches such ardors from me I did not know I
	possess'd them,
It sails me, I dab with bare feet, they are lick'd by the
	indolent waves,
I am cut by bitter and angry hail, I lose my breath,
Steep'd amid honey'd morphine, my windpipe throttled
	in fakes of death,
At length let up again to feel the puzzle of puzzles,
And that we call Being.

27

To be in any form, what is that?
(Round and round we go, all of us, and ever come back
	thither,)
If nothing lay more develop'd the quahaug in its callous
	shell were enough.

Mine is no callous shell,
I have instant conductors all over me whether I pass
	or stop,
They seize every object and lead it harmlessly
	through me.

I merely stir, press, feel with my fingers, and am happy,
To touch my person to some one else's is about as much
	as I can stand.

28

Is this then a touch? quivering me to a new identity,
Flames and ether making a rush for my veins,
Treacherous tip of me reaching and crowding to help
    them,
My flesh and blood playing out lightning to strike what
    is hardly different from myself,
On all sides prurient provokers stiffening my limbs,
Straining the udder of my heart for its withheld drip,
Behaving licentious toward me, taking no denial,
Depriving me of my best as for a purpose,
Unbuttoning my clothes, holding me by the bare waist,
Deluding my confusion with the calm of the sunlight
    and pasture-fields,
Immodestly sliding the fellow-senses away,
They bribed to swap off with touch and go and graze at
    the edges of me,
No consideration, no regard for my draining strength or
    my anger,
Fetching the rest of the herd around to enjoy them
    a while,
Then all uniting to stand on a headland and worry me.

The sentries desert every other part of me,
They have left me helpless to a red marauder,
They all come to the headland to witness and assist
    against me.

I am given up by traitors,
I talk wildly, I have lost my wits, I and nobody else am
    the greatest traitor,

I went myself first to the headland, my own hands
        carried me there.

You villain touch! what are you doing? my breath is
        tight in its throat,
Unclench your floodgates, you are too much for me.

29

Blind loving wrestling touch, sheath'd hooded
        sharp-tooth'd touch!
Did it make you ache so, leaving me?

Parting track'd by arriving, perpetual payment of
        perpetual loan,
Rich showering rain, and recompense richer afterward.

Sprouts take and accumulate, stand by the curb prolific
        and vital,
Landscapes projected masculine, full-sized and golden.

30

All truths wait in all things,
They neither hasten their own delivery nor resist it,
They do not need the obstetric forceps of the surgeon,
The insignificant is as big to me as any,
(What is less or more than a touch?)

Logic and sermons never convince,
The damp of the night drives deeper into my soul.

(Only what proves itself to every man and woman is so,
Only what nobody denies is so.)

A minute and a drop of me settle my brain,
I believe the soggy clods shall become lovers and lamps,
And a compend of compends is the meat of a man or
    woman,
And a summit and flower there is the feeling they have
    for each other,
And they are to branch boundlessly out of that lesson
    until it becomes omnific,
And until one and all shall delight us, and we them.

31

I believe a leaf of grass is no less than the journey-work
    of the stars,
And the pismire is equally perfect, and a grain of sand,
    and the egg of the wren,
And the tree-toad is a chef-d'œuvre for the highest,
And the running blackberry would adorn the parlors of
    heaven,
And the narrowest hinge in my hand puts to scorn all
    machinery,
And the cow crunching with depress'd head surpasses
    any statue,
And a mouse is miracle enough to stagger sextillions of
    infidels.

I find I incorporate gneiss, coal, long-threaded moss,
    fruits, grains, esculent roots,
And am stucco'd with quadrupeds and birds all over,

And have distanced what is behind me for good reasons,
But call any thing back again when I desire it.

In vain the speeding or shyness,
In vain the plutonic rocks send their old heat against my
      approach,
In vain the mastodon retreats beneath its own powder'd
      bones,
In vain objects stand leagues off and assume manifold
      shapes,
In vain the ocean settling in hollows and the great
      monsters lying low,
In vain the buzzard houses herself with the sky,
In vain the snake slides through the creepers and logs,
In vain the elk takes to the inner passes of the woods,
In vain the razor-bill'd auk sails far north to Labrador,
I follow quickly, I ascend to the nest in the fissure of
      the cliff.

32

I think I could turn and live with animals, they are so
      placid and self-contain'd,
I stand and look at them long and long.

They do not sweat and whine about their condition,
They do not lie awake in the dark and weep for their
      sins,
They do not make me sick discussing their duty to God,
Not one is dissatisfied, not one is demented with the
      mania of owning things,

Not one kneels to another, nor to his kind that lived
    thousands of years ago,
Not one is respectable or unhappy over the whole earth.

So they show their relations to me and I accept them,
They bring me tokens of myself, they evince them
    plainly in their possession.

I wonder where they get those tokens,
Did I pass that way huge times ago and negligently drop
    them?

Myself moving forward then and now and forever,
Gathering and showing more always and with velocity,
Infinite and omnigenous, and the like of these among
    them,
Not too exclusive toward the reachers of my
    remembrancers,
Picking out here one that I love, and now go with him
    on brotherly terms.

A gigantic beauty of a stallion, fresh and responsive to
    my caresses,
Head high in the forehead, wide between the ears,
Limbs glossy and supple, tail dusting the ground,
Eyes full of sparkling wickedness, ears finely cut, flexibly
    moving.

His nostrils dilate as my heels embrace him,
His well-built limbs tremble with pleasure as we race
    around and return.

I but use you a minute, then I resign you, stallion,
Why do I need your paces when I myself out-gallop
    them?
Even as I stand or sit passing faster than you.

33

Space and Time! now I see it is true, what I guess'd at,
What I guess'd when I loaf'd on the grass,
What I guess'd while I lay alone in my bed,
And again as I walk'd the beach under the paling stars of
    the morning.

My ties and ballasts leave me, my elbows rest in
    sea-gaps,
I skirt sierras, my palms cover continents,
I am afoot with my vision.

By the city's quadrangular houses—in log huts, camping
    with lumbermen,
Along the ruts of the turnpike, along the dry gulch and
    rivulet bed,
Weeding my onion-patch or hoeing rows of carrots and
    parsnips, crossing savannas, trailing in forests,
Prospecting, gold-digging, girdling the trees of a new
    purchase,
Scorch'd ankle-deep by the hot sand, hauling my boat
    down the shallow river,
Where the panther walks to and fro on a limb overhead,
    where the buck turns furiously at the hunter,
Where the rattlesnake suns his flabby length on a rock,
    where the otter is feeding on fish,

Where the alligator in his tough pimples sleeps by
	the bayou,
Where the black bear is searching for roots or honey,
	where the beaver pats the mud with his paddle-
	shaped tail;
Over the growing sugar, over the yellow-flower'd cotton
	plant, over the rice in its low moist field,
Over the sharp-peak'd farm house, with its scallop'd
	scum and slender shoots from the gutters,
Over the western persimmon, over the long-leav'd corn,
	over the delicate blue-flower flax,
Over the white and brown buckwheat, a hummer and
	buzzer there with the rest,
Over the dusky green of the rye as it ripples and shades
	in the breeze;
Scaling mountains, pulling myself cautiously up,
	holding on by low scragged limbs,
Walking the path worn in the grass and beat through
	the leaves of the brush,
Where the quail is whistling betwixt the woods and the
	wheat-lot,
Where the bat flies in the Seventh-month eve, where
	the great goldbug drops through the dark,
Where the brook puts out of the roots of the old tree
	and flows to the meadow,
Where cattle stand and shake away flies with the
	tremulous shuddering of their hides,
Where the cheese-cloth hangs in the kitchen, where
	andirons straddle the hearth-slab, where cobwebs
	fall in festoons from the rafters;
Where trip-hammers crash, where the press is whirling
	its cylinders,

Wherever the human heart beats with terrible throes
     under its ribs,
Where the pear-shaped balloon is floating aloft,
     (floating in it myself and looking composedly down,)
Where the life-car is drawn on the slip-noose, where the
     heat hatches pale-green eggs in the dented sand,
Where the she-whale swims with her calf and never
     forsakes it,
Where the steam-ship trails hind-ways its long pennant
     of smoke,
Where the fin of the shark cuts like a black chip out of
     the water,
Where the half-burn'd brig is riding on unknown
     currents,
Where shells grow to her slimy deck, where the dead
     are corrupting below;
Where the dense-starr'd flag is borne at the head of the
     regiments,
Approaching Manhattan up by the long-stretching
     island,
Under Niagara, the cataract falling like a veil over my
     countenance,
Upon a door-step, upon the horse-block of hard wood
     outside,
Upon the race-course, or enjoying picnics or jigs or a
     good game of base-ball,
At he-festivals, with blackguard gibes, ironical license,
     bull-dances, drinking, laughter,
At the cider-mill tasting the sweets of the brown mash,
     sucking the juice through a straw,
At apple-peelings wanting kisses for all the red fruit
     I find,

At musters, beach-parties, friendly bees, huskings,
    house-raisings;
Where the mocking-bird sounds his delicious gurgles,
    cackles, screams, weeps,
Where the hay-rick stands in the barn-yard, where the
    dry-stalks are scatter'd, where the brood-cow waits
    in the hovel,
Where the bull advances to do his masculine work,
    where the stud to the mare, where the cock is
    treading the hen,
Where the heifers browse, where geese nip their food
    with short jerks,
Where sun-down shadows lengthen over the limitless
    and lonesome prairie,
Where herds of buffalo make a crawling spread of the
    square miles far and near,
Where the humming-bird shimmers, where the neck of
    the long-lived swan is curving and winding,
Where the laughing-gull scoots by the shore, where she
    laughs her near-human laugh,
Where bee-hives range on a gray bench in the garden
    half hid by the high weeds,
Where band-neck'd partridges roost in a ring on the
    ground with their heads out,
Where burial coaches enter the arch'd gates of a
    cemetery,
Where winter wolves bark amid wastes of snow and
    icicled trees,
Where the yellow-crown'd heron comes to the edge
    of the marsh at night and feeds upon small crabs,
Where the splash of swimmers and divers cools the
    warm noon,

Where the katy-did works her chromatic reed on the
      walnut-tree over the well,
Through patches of citrons and cucumbers with
      silver-wired leaves,
Through the salt-lick or orange glade, or under
      conical firs,
Through the gymnasium, through the curtain'd saloon,
      through the office or public hall;
Pleas'd with the native and pleas'd with the foreign,
      pleas'd with the new and old,
Pleas'd with the homely woman as well as the handsome,
Pleas'd with the quakeress as she puts off her bonnet
      and talks melodiously,
Pleas'd with the tune of the choir of the whitewash'd
      church,
Pleas'd with the earnest words of the sweating
      Methodist preacher, impress'd seriously at the
      camp-meeting;
Looking in at the shop-windows of Broadway the whole
      forenoon, flatting the flesh of my nose on the thick
      plate glass,
Wandering the same afternoon with my face turn'd up
      to the clouds, or down a lane or along the beach,
My right and left arms round the sides of two friends,
      and I in the middle;
Coming home with the silent and dark-cheek'd
      bush-boy, (behind me he rides at the drape of
      the day,)
Far from the settlements studying the print of animals'
      feet, or the moccasin print,
By the cot in the hospital reaching lemonade to a
      feverish patient,

Nigh the coffin'd corpse when all is still, examining with
a candle;
Voyaging to every port to dicker and adventure,
Hurrying with the modern crowd as eager and fickle
as any,
Hot toward one I hate, ready in my madness to knife
him,
Solitary at midnight in my back yard, my thoughts gone
from me a long while,
Walking the old hills of Judæa with the beautiful gentle
God by my side,
Speeding through space, speeding through heaven and
the stars,
Speeding amid the seven satellites and the broad ring,
and the diameter of eighty thousand miles,
Speeding with tail'd meteors, throwing fire-balls like
the rest,
Carrying the crescent child that carries its own full
mother in its belly,
Storming, enjoying, planning, loving, cautioning,
Backing and filling, appearing and disappearing,
I tread day and night such roads.

I visit the orchards of spheres and look at the product,
And look at quintillions ripen'd and look at quintillions
green.

I fly those flights of a fluid and swallowing soul,
My course runs below the soundings of plummets.

I help myself to material and immaterial,
No guard can shut me off, no law prevent me.

I anchor my ship for a little while only,
My messengers continually cruise away or bring their
      returns to me.

I go hunting polar furs and the seal, leaping chasms with
      a pike-pointed staff, clinging to topples of brittle
      and blue.

I ascend to the foretruck,
I take my place late at night in the crow's-nest,
We sail the arctic sea, it is plenty light enough,
Through the clear atmosphere I stretch around on the
      wonderful beauty,
The enormous masses of ice pass me and I pass them,
      the scenery is plain in all directions,
The white-topt mountains show in the distance, I fling
      out my fancies toward them,
We are approaching some great battle-field in which we
      are soon to be engaged,
We pass the colossal outposts of the encampment, we
      pass with still feet and caution,
Or we are entering by the suburbs some vast and ruin'd
      city,
The blocks and fallen architecture more than all the
      living cities of the globe.

I am a free companion, I bivouac by invading
      watchfires,
I turn the bridegroom out of bed and stay with the bride
      myself,
I tighten her all night to my thighs and lips.

My voice is the wife's voice, the screech by the rail of
    the stairs,
They fetch my man's body up dripping and drown'd.

I understand the large hearts of heroes,
The courage of present times and all times,
How the skipper saw the crowded and rudderless wreck
    of the steam-ship, and Death chasing it up and
    down the storm,
How he knuckled tight and gave not back an inch, and
    was faithful of days and faithful of nights,
And chalk'd in large letters on a board, *Be of good cheer,*
    we will not desert you;
How he follow'd with them and tack'd with them three
    days and would not give it up,
How he saved the drifting company at last,
How the lank loose-gown'd women look'd when boated
    from the side of their prepared graves,
How the silent old-faced infants and the lifted sick, and
    the sharp-lipp'd unshaved men;
All this I swallow, it tastes good, I like it well, it
    becomes mine,
I am the man, I suffer'd, I was there.

The disdain and calmness of martyrs,
The mother of old, condemn'd for a witch, burnt with
    dry wood, her children gazing on,
The hounded slave that flags in the race, leans by the
    fence, blowing, cover'd with sweat,
The twinges that sting like needles his legs and neck,
    the murderous buckshot and the bullets,
All these I feel or am.

I am the hounded slave, I wince at the bite of the dogs,
Hell and despair are upon me, crack and again crack the
    marksmen,
I clutch the rails of the fence, my gore dribs, thinn'd
    with the ooze of my skin,
I fall on the weeds and stones,
The riders spur their unwilling horses, haul close,
Taunt my dizzy ears and beat me violently over the head
    with whip-stocks.

Agonies are one of my changes of garments,
I do not ask the wounded person how he feels, I myself
    become the wounded person,
My hurts turn livid upon me as I lean on a cane and
    observe.

I am the mash'd fireman with breast-bone broken,
Tumbling walls buried me in their debris,
Heat and smoke I inspired, I heard the yelling shouts of
    my comrades,
I heard the distant click of their picks and shovels,
They have clear'd the beams away, they tenderly lift
    me forth.

I lie in the night air in my red shirt, the pervading hush
    is for my sake,
Painless after all I lie exhausted but not so unhappy,
White and beautiful are the faces around me, the heads
    are bared of their fire-caps,
The kneeling crowd fades with the light of the torches.

Distant and dead resuscitate,
They show as the dial or move as the hands of me, I am
    the clock myself.

I am an old artillerist, I tell of my fort's bombardment,
I am there again.

Again the long roll of the drummers,
Again the attacking cannon, mortars,
Again to my listening ears the cannon responsive.

I take part, I see and hear the whole,
The cries, curses, roar, the plaudits for well-aim'd shots,
The ambulanza slowly passing trailing its red drip,
Workmen searching after damages, making
    indispensable repairs,
The fall of grenades through the rent roof, the
    fan-shaped explosion,
The whizz of limbs, heads, stone, wood, iron, high in
    the air.

Again gurgles the mouth of my dying general, he
    furiously waves with his hand,
He gasps through the clot *Mind not me—mind—the
entrenchments.*

34

Now I tell what I knew in Texas in my early youth,
(I tell not the fall of Alamo,
Not one escaped to tell the fall of Alamo,
The hundred and fifty are dumb yet at Alamo,)
'Tis the tale of the murder in cold blood of four
    hundred and twelve young men.

Retreating they had form'd in a hollow square with their
      baggage for breastworks,
Nine hundred lives out of the surrounding enemy's,
      nine times their number, was the price they took in
      advance,
Their colonel was wounded and their ammunition gone,
They treated for an honorable capitulation, receiv'd
      writing and seal, gave up their arms and march'd
      back prisoners of war.

They were the glory of the race of rangers,
Matchless with horse, rifle, song, supper, courtship,
Large, turbulent, generous, handsome, proud, and
      affectionate,
Bearded, sunburnt, drest in the free costume of hunters,
Not a single one over thirty years of age.

The second First-day morning they were brought out
      in squads and massacred, it was beautiful early
      summer,
The work commenced about five o'clock and was over
      by eight.

None obey'd the command to kneel,
Some made a mad and helpless rush, some stood stark
      and straight,
A few fell at once, shot in the temple or heart, the living
      and dead lay together,
The maim'd and mangled dug in the dirt, the new-
      comers saw them there,
Some half-kill'd attempted to crawl away,

These were despatch'd with bayonets or batter'd with
    the blunts of muskets,
A youth not seventeen years old seiz'd his assassin till
    two more came to release him,
The three were all torn and cover'd with the boy's
    blood.

At eleven o'clock began the burning of the bodies;
That is the tale of the murder of the four hundred and
    twelve young men.

35

Would you hear of an old-time sea-fight?
Would you learn who won by the light of the moon and
    stars?
List to the yarn, as my grandmother's father the sailor
    told it to me.

Our foe was no skulk in his ship I tell you, (said he,)
His was the surly English pluck, and there is no tougher
    or truer, and never was, and never will be;
Along the lower'd eve he came horribly raking us.

We closed with him, the yards entangled, the cannon
    touch'd,
My captain lash'd fast with his own hands.

We had receiv'd some eighteen pound shots under the
    water,
On our lower-gun-deck two large pieces had burst at
    the first fire, killing all around and blowing up
    overhead.

Fighting at sun-down, fighting at dark,
Ten o'clock at night, the full moon well up, our leaks on
      the gain, and five feet of water reported,
The master-at-arms loosing the prisoners confined in
      the after-hold to give them a chance for themselves.

The transit to and from the magazine is now stopt by
      the sentinels,
They see so many strange faces they do not know whom
      to trust.

Our frigate takes fire,
The other asks if we demand quarter?
If our colors are struck and the fighting done?

Now I laugh content, for I hear the voice of my little
      captain,
We have not struck, he composedly cries, *we have just
      begun our part of the fighting.*

Only three guns are in use,
One is directed by the captain himself against the
      enemy's mainmast,
Two well serv'd with grape and canister silence his
      musketry and clear his decks.

The tops alone second the fire of this little battery,
      especially the main-top,
They hold out bravely during the whole of the action.

Not a moment's cease,
The leaks gain fast on the pumps, the fire eats toward
      the powder-magazine.

One of the pumps has been shot away, it is generally
    thought we are sinking.

Serene stands the little captain,
He is not hurried, his voice is neither high nor low,
His eyes give more light to us than our battle-lanterns.

Toward twelve there in the beams of the moon they
    surrender to us.

36

Stretch'd and still lies the midnight,
Two great hulls motionless on the breast of the darkness,
Our vessel riddled and slowly sinking, preparations to
    pass to the one we have conquer'd,
The captain on the quarter-deck coldly giving his orders
    through a countenance white as a sheet,
Near by the corpse of the child that serv'd in the cabin,
The dead face of an old salt with long white hair and
    carefully curl'd whiskers,
The flames spite of all that can be done flickering aloft
    and below,
The husky voices of the two or three officers yet fit for
    duty,
Formless stacks of bodies and bodies by themselves,
    dabs of flesh upon the masts and spars,
Cut of cordage, dangle of rigging, slight shock of the
    soothe of waves,
Black and impassive guns, litter of powder-parcels,
    strong scent,
A few large stars overhead, silent and mournful shining,

Delicate sniffs of sea-breeze, smells of sedgy grass and
    fields by the shore, death-messages given in charge
    to survivors,
The hiss of the surgeon's knife, the gnawing teeth of
    his saw,
Wheeze, cluck, swash of falling blood, short wild
    scream, and long, dull, tapering groan,
These so, these irretrievable.

37

You laggards there on guard! look to your arms!
In at the conquer'd doors they crowd! I am possess'd!
Embody all presences outlaw'd or suffering,
See myself in prison shaped like another man,
And feel the dull unintermitted pain.

For me the keepers of convicts shoulder their carbines
    and keep watch,
It is I let out in the morning and barr'd at night.

Not a mutineer walks handcuff'd to jail but I am
    handcuff'd to him and walk by his side,
(I am less the jolly one there, and more the silent one
    with sweat on my twitching lips.)

Not a youngster is taken for larceny but I go up too, and
    am tried and sentenced.

Not a cholera patient lies at the last gasp but I also lie at
    the last gasp,
My face is ash-color'd, my sinews gnarl, away from me
    people retreat.

Askers embody themselves in me and I am embodied
    in them,
I project my hat, sit shame-faced, and beg.

38

Enough! enough! enough!
Somehow I have been stunn'd. Stand back!
Give me a little time beyond my cuff'd head, slumbers,
    dreams, gaping,
I discover myself on the verge of a usual mistake.

That I could forget the mockers and insults!
That I could forget the trickling tears and the blows of
    the bludgeons and hammers!
That I could look with a separate look on my own
    crucifixion and bloody crowning.

I remember now,
I resume the overstaid fraction,
The grave of rock multiplies what has been confided to
    it, or to any graves,
Corpses rise, gashes heal, fastenings roll from me.

I troop forth replenish'd with supreme power, one of an
    average unending procession,
Inland and sea-coast we go, and pass all boundary lines,
Our swift ordinances on their way over the whole earth,
The blossoms we wear in our hats the growth of
    thousands of years.

Eleves, I salute you! come forward!
Continue your annotations, continue your
    questionings.

39

The friendly and flowing savage, who is he?
Is he waiting for civilization, or past it and mastering it?

Is he some Southwesterner rais'd out-doors? is he
    Kanadian?
Is he from the Mississippi country? Iowa, Oregon,
    California?
The mountains? prairie-life, bush-life? or sailor from
    the sea?

Wherever he goes men and women accept and
    desire him,
They desire he should like them, touch them, speak to
    them, stay with them.

Behavior lawless as snow-flakes, words simple as grass,
    uncomb'd head, laughter, and naivetè,
Slow-stepping feet, common features, common modes
    and emanations,
They descend in new forms from the tips of his fingers,
They are wafted with the odor of his body or breath,
    they fly out of the glance of his eyes.

40

Flaunt of the sunshine I need not your bask—lie over!
You light surfaces only, I force surfaces and depths also.

Earth! you seem to look for something at my hands,
Say, old top-knot, what do you want?

Man or woman, I might tell how I like you, but cannot,
And might tell what it is in me and what it is in you, but
    cannot,
And might tell that pining I have, that pulse of my
    nights and days.

Behold, I do not give lectures or a little charity,
When I give I give myself.

You there, impotent, loose in the knees,
Open your scarf'd chops till I blow grit within you,
Spread your palms and lift the flaps of your pockets,
I am not to be denied, I compel, I have stores plenty and
    to spare,
And any thing I have I bestow.

I do not ask who you are, that is not important to me,
You can do nothing and be nothing but what I will
    infold you.

To cotton-field drudge or cleaner of privies I lean,
On his right cheek I put the family kiss,
And in my soul I swear I never will deny him.

On women fit for conception I start bigger and nimbler
    babes,
(This day I am jetting the stuff of far more arrogant
    republics.)

To any one dying, thither I speed and twist the knob of
    the door,
Turn the bed-clothes toward the foot of the bed,
Let the physician and the priest go home.

I seize the descending man and raise him with
    resistless will,
O despairer, here is my neck,
By God, you shall not go down! hang your whole
    weight upon me.

I dilate you with tremendous breath, I buoy you up,
Every room of the house do I fill with an arm'd force,
Lovers of me, bafflers of graves.

Sleep—I and they keep guard all night,
Not doubt, not decease shall dare to lay finger upon you,
I have embraced you, and henceforth possess you to
    myself,
And when you rise in the morning you will find what I
    tell you is so.

41

I am he bringing help for the sick as they pant on
    their backs,
And for strong upright men I bring yet more
    needed help.

I heard what was said of the universe,
Heard it and heard it of several thousand years;
It is middling well as far as it goes—but is that all?

Magnifying and applying come I,
Outbidding at the start the old cautious hucksters,
Taking myself the exact dimensions of Jehovah,
Lithographing Kronos, Zeus his son, and Hercules his
    grandson,

Buying drafts of Osiris, Isis, Belus, Brahma, Buddha,
In my portfolio placing Manito loose, Allah on a leaf,
    the crucifix engraved,
With Odin and the hideous-faced Mexitli and every idol
    and image,
Taking them all for what they are worth and not a cent
    more,
Admitting they were alive and did the work of their days,
(They bore mites as for unfledg'd birds who have now
    to rise and fly and sing for themselves,)
Accepting the rough deific sketches to fill out better in
    myself, bestowing them freely on each man and
    woman I see,
Discovering as much or more in a framer framing a
    house,
Putting higher claims for him there with his roll'd-up
    sleeves driving the mallet and chisel,
Not objecting to special revelations, considering a curl
    of smoke or a hair on the back of my hand just as
    curious as any revelation,
Lads ahold of fire-engines and hook-and-ladder ropes
    no less to me than the gods of the antique wars,
Minding their voices peal through the crash of
    destruction,
Their brawny limbs passing safe over charr'd laths, their
    white foreheads whole and unhurt out of the
    flames;
By the mechanic's wife with her babe at her nipple
    interceding for every person born,
Three scythes at harvest whizzing in a row from three
    lusty angels with shirts bagg'd out at their waists,

The snag-tooth'd hostler with red hair redeeming sins
    past and to come,
Selling all he possesses, traveling on foot to fee lawyers
    for his brother and sit by him while he is tried for
    forgery;
What was strewn in the amplest strewing the square rod
    about me, and not filling the square rod then,
The bull and the bug never worshipp'd half enough,
Dung and dirt more admirable than was dream'd,
The supernatural of no account, myself waiting my time
    to be one of the supremes,
The day getting ready for me when I shall do as much
    good as the best, and be as prodigious;
By my life-lumps! becoming already a creator,
Putting myself here and now to the ambush'd womb of
    the shadows.

42

A call in the midst of the crowd,
My own voice, orotund sweeping and final.

Come my children,
Come my boys and girls, my women, household and
    intimates,
Now the performer launches his nerve, he has pass'd his
    prelude on the reeds within.

Easily written loose-finger'd chords—I feel the thrum of
    your climax and close.

My head slues round on my neck,
Music rolls, but not from the organ,
Folks are around me, but they are no household of mine.

Ever the hard unsunk ground,
Ever the eaters and drinkers, ever the upward and
    downward sun, ever the air and the ceaseless tides,
Ever myself and my neighbors, refreshing, wicked, real,
Ever the old inexplicable query, ever that thorn'd
    thumb, that breath of itches and thirsts,
Ever the vexer's *hoot! hoot!* till we find where the sly one
    hides and bring him forth,
Ever love, ever the sobbing liquid of life,
Ever the bandage under the chin, ever the trestles
    of death.

Here and there with dimes on the eyes walking,
To feed the greed of the belly the brains liberally
    spooning,
Tickets buying, taking, selling, but in to the feast never
    once going.
Many sweating, ploughing, thrashing, and then the
    chaff for payment receiving,
A few idly owning, and they the wheat continually
    claiming.

This is the city and I am one of the citizens,
Whatever interests the rest interests me, politics, wars,
    markets, newspapers, schools,
The mayor and councils, banks, tariffs, steamships,
    factories, stocks, stores, real estate and personal
    estate.

The little plentiful manikins skipping around in collars
and tail'd coats,
I am aware who they are, (they are positively not worms
or fleas,)
I acknowledge the duplicates of myself, the weakest and
shallowest is deathless with me,
What I do and say the same waits for them,
Every thought that flounders in me the same flounders
in them.

I know perfectly well my own egotism,
Know my omnivorous lines and must not write any less,
And would fetch you whoever you are flush with myself.

Not words of routine this song of mine,
But abruptly to question, to leap beyond yet nearer
bring;
This printed and bound book—but the printer and the
printing-office boy?
The well-taken photographs—but your wife or friend
close and solid in your arms?
The black ship mail'd with iron, her mighty guns in her
turrets—but the pluck of the captain and
engineers?
In the houses the dishes and fare and furniture—but the
host and hostess, and the look out of their eyes?
The sky up there—yet here or next door, or across
the way?
The saints and sages in history—but you yourself?
Sermons, creeds, theology—but the fathomless human
brain,
And what is reason? and what is love? and what is life?

43

I do not despise you priests, all time, the world over,
My faith is the greatest of faiths and the least of faiths,
Enclosing worship ancient and modern and all between
    ancient and modern,
Believing I shall come again upon the earth after five
    thousand years,
Waiting responses from oracles, honoring the gods,
    saluting the sun,
Making a fetich of the first rock or stump, powowing
    with sticks in the circle of obis,
Helping the llama or brahmin as he trims the lamps of
    the idols,
Dancing yet through the streets in a phallic procession,
    rapt and austere in the woods a gymnosophist,
Drinking mead from the skull-cup, to Shastas and Vedas
    admirant, minding the Koran,
Walking the teokallis, spotted with gore from the stone
    and knife, beating the serpent-skin drum,
Accepting the Gospels, accepting him that was crucified,
    knowing assuredly that he is divine,
To the mass kneeling or the puritan's prayer rising, or
    sitting patiently in a pew,
Ranting and frothing in my insane crisis, or waiting
    dead-like till my spirit arouses me,
Looking forth on pavement and land, or outside of
    pavement and land,
Belonging to the winders of the circuit of circuits.

One of that centripetal and centrifugal gang I turn and
    talk like a man leaving charges before a journey.

Down-hearted doubters dull and excluded,
Frivolous, sullen, moping, angry, affected, dishearten'd,
    atheistical,
I know every one of you, I know the sea of torment,
    doubt, despair and unbelief.

How the flukes splash!
How they contort rapid as lightning, with spasms and
    spouts of blood!

Be at peace bloody flukes of doubters and sullen mopers,
I take my place among you as much as among any,
The past is the push of you, me, all, precisely the same,
And what is yet untried and afterward is for you, me, all,
    precisely the same.

I do not know what is untried and afterward,
But I know it will in its turn prove sufficient, and
    cannot fail.

Each who passes is consider'd, each who stops is
    consider'd, not a single one can it fail.

It cannot fail the young man who died and was buried,
Nor the young woman who died and was put by his side,
Nor the little child that peep'd in at the door, and then
    drew back and was never seen again,
Nor the old man who has lived without purpose, and
    feels it with bitterness worse than gall,
Nor him in the poor house tubercled by rum and the
    bad disorder,

Nor the numberless slaughter'd and wreck'd, nor the
    brutish koboo call'd the ordure of humanity,
Nor the sacs merely floating with open mouths for food
    to slip in,
Nor any thing in the earth, or down in the oldest graves
    of the earth,
Nor any thing in the myriads of spheres, nor the
    myriads of myriads that inhabit them,
Nor the present, nor the least wisp that is known.

44

It is time to explain myself—let us stand up.

What is known I strip away,
I launch all men and women forward with me into the
    Unknown.

The clock indicates the moment—but what does
    eternity indicate?

We have thus far exhausted trillions of winters and
    summers,
There are trillions ahead, and trillions ahead of them.

Births have brought us richness and variety,
And other births will bring us richness and variety.

I do not call one greater and one smaller,
That which fills its period and place is equal to any.

Were mankind murderous or jealous upon you, my
      brother, my sister?
I am sorry for you, they are not murderous or jealous
      upon me,
All has been gentle with me, I keep no account with
      lamentation,
(What have I to do with lamentation?)

I am an acme of things accomplish'd, and I an encloser
      of things to be.

My feet strike an apex of the apices of the stairs,
On every step bunches of ages, and larger bunches
      between the steps,
All below duly travel'd, and still I mount and mount.

Rise after rise bow the phantoms behind me,
Afar down I see the huge first Nothing, I know I was
      even there,
I waited unseen and always, and slept through the
      lethargic mist,
And took my time, and took no hurt from the fetid
      carbon.

Long I was hugg'd close—long and long.

Immense have been the preparations for me,
Faithful and friendly the arms that have help'd me.

Cycles ferried my cradle, rowing and rowing like
      cheerful boatmen,
For room to me stars kept aside in their own rings,
They sent influences to look after what was to hold me.

Before I was born out of my mother generations
    guided me,
My embryo has never been torpid, nothing could
    overlay it.

For it the nebula cohered to an orb,
The long slow strata piled to rest it on,
Vast vegetables gave it sustenance,
Monstrous sauroids transported it in their mouths and
    deposited it with care.

All forces have been steadily employ'd to complete and
    delight me,
Now on this spot I stand with my robust soul.

45

O span of youth! ever-push'd elasticity!
O manhood, balanced, florid and full.

My lovers suffocate me,
Crowding my lips, thick in the pores of my skin,
Jostling me through streets and public halls, coming
    naked to me at night,
Crying by day *Ahoy!* from the rocks of the river,
    swinging and chirping over my head,
Calling my name from flower-beds, vines, tangled
    underbrush,
Lighting on every moment of my life,
Bussing my body with soft balsamic busses,
Noiselessly passing handfuls out of their hearts and
    giving them to be mine.

Old age superbly rising! O welcome, ineffable grace of
    dying days!

Every condition promulges not only itself, it promulges
    what grows after and out of itself,
And the dark hush promulges as much as any.

I open my scuttle at night and see the far-sprinkled
    systems,
And all I see multiplied as high as I can cipher edge but
    the rim of the farther systems.

Wider and wider they spread, expanding, always
    expanding,
Outward and outward and forever outward.

My sun has his sun and round him obediently
    wheels,
He joins with his partners a group of superior circuit,
And greater sets follow, making specks of the greatest
    inside them.

There is no stoppage and never can be stoppage,
If I, you, and the worlds, and all beneath or upon their
    surfaces, were this moment reduced back to a pallid
    float, it would not avail in the long run,
We should surely bring up again where we now stand,
And surely go as much farther, and then farther and
    farther.

A few quadrillions of eras, a few octillions of cubic
    leagues, do not hazard the span or make it
    impatient,
They are but parts, any thing is but a part.

See ever so far, there is limitless space outside of that,
Count ever so much, there is limitless time around that.

My rendezvous is appointed, it is certain,
The Lord will be there and wait till I come on perfect
    terms,
The great Camerado, the lover true for whom I pine
    will be there.

46

I know I have the best of time and space, and was never
    measured and never will be measured.

I tramp a perpetual journey, (come listen all!)
My signs are a rain-proof coat, good shoes, and a staff
    cut from the woods,
No friend of mine takes his ease in my chair,
I have no chair, no church, no philosophy,
I lead no man to a dinner-table, library, exchange,
But each man and each woman of you I lead upon a knoll,
My left hand hooking you round the waist,
My right hand pointing to landscapes of continents and
    the public road.

Not I, not any one else can travel that road for you,
You must travel it for yourself.

It is not far, it is within reach,
Perhaps you have been on it since you were born and
     did not know,
Perhaps it is everywhere on water and on land.

Shoulder your duds dear son, and I will mine, and let us
     hasten forth,
Wonderful cities and free nations we shall fetch as we go.

If you tire, give me both burdens, and rest the chuff of
     your hand on my hip,
And in due time you shall repay the same service to me,
For after we start we never lie by again.

This day before dawn I ascended a hill and look'd at the
     crowded heaven,
And I said to my spirit *When we become the enfolders of
     those orbs, and the pleasure and knowledge of every
     thing in them, shall we be fill'd and satisfied then?*
And my spirit said *No, we but level that lift to pass and
     continue beyond.*

You are also asking me questions and I hear you,
I answer that I cannot answer, you must find out for
     yourself.

Sit a while dear son,
Here are biscuits to eat and here is milk to drink,
But as soon as you sleep and renew yourself in sweet
     clothes, I kiss you with a good-by kiss and open the
     gate for your egress hence.

Long enough have you dream'd contemptible dreams,
Now I wash the gum from your eyes,
You must habit yourself to the dazzle of the light and of
every moment of your life.

Long have you timidly waded holding a plank by the
shore,
Now I will you to be a bold swimmer,
To jump off in the midst of the sea, rise again, nod to
me, shout, and laughingly dash with your hair.

47

I am the teacher of athletes,
He that by me spreads a wider breast than my own
proves the width of my own,
He most honors my style who learns under it to destroy
the teacher.

The boy I love, the same becomes a man not through
derived power, but in his own right,
Wicked rather than virtuous out of conformity
or fear,
Fond of his sweetheart, relishing well his steak,
Unrequited love or a slight cutting him worse than
sharp steel cuts,
First-rate to ride, to fight, to hit the bull's eye, to sail a
skiff, to sing a song or play on the banjo,
Preferring scars and the beard and faces pitted with
small-pox over all latherers,
And those well-tann'd to those that keep out of
the sun.

I teach straying from me, yet who can stray from me?
I follow you whoever you are from the present hour,
My words itch at your ears till you understand them.

I do not say these things for a dollar or to fill up the
        time while I wait for a boat,
(It is you talking just as much as myself, I act as the
        tongue of you,
Tied in your mouth, in mine it begins to be loosen'd.)

I swear I will never again mention love or death inside a
        house,
And I swear I will never translate myself at all, only to
        him or her who privately stays with me in the
        open air.

If you would understand me go to the heights or
        water-shore,
The nearest gnat is an explanation, and a drop or
        motion of waves a key,
The maul, the oar, the hand-saw, second my words.

No shutter'd room or school can commune with me,
But roughs and little children better than they.

The young mechanic is closest to me, he knows
        me well,
The woodman that takes his axe and jug with him shall
        take me with him all day,
The farm-boy ploughing in the field feels good at the
        sound of my voice,
In vessels that sail my words sail, I go with fishermen
        and seamen and love them.

The soldier camp'd or upon the march is mine,
On the night ere the pending battle many seek me, and
      I do not fail them,
On that solemn night (it may be their last) those that
      know me seek me.

My face rubs to the hunter's face when he lies down
      alone in his blanket,
The driver thinking of me does not mind the jolt of his
      wagon,
The young mother and old mother comprehend me,
The girl and the wife rest the needle a moment and for-
      get where they are,
They and all would resume what I have told them.

48

I have said that the soul is not more than the body,
And I have said that the body is not more than the soul,
And nothing, not God, is greater to one than one's
      self is,
And whoever walks a furlong without sympathy walks to
      his own funeral drest in his shroud,
And I or you pocketless of a dime may purchase the pick
      of the earth,
And to glance with an eye or show a bean in its pod
      confounds the learning of all times,
And there is no trade or employment but the young
      man following it may become a hero,
And there is no object so soft but it makes a hub for the
      wheel'd universe,
And I say to any man or woman, Let your soul stand
      cool and composed before a million universes.

And I say to mankind, Be not curious about God,
For I who am curious about each am not curious
    about God,
(No array of terms can say how much I am at peace
    about God and about death.)

I hear and behold God in every object, yet understand
    God not in the least,
Nor do I understand who there can be more wonderful
    than myself.

Why should I wish to see God better than this day?
I see something of God each hour of the twenty-four,
    and each moment then,
In the faces of men and women I see God, and in my
    own face in the glass,
I find letters from God dropt in the street, and every
    one is sign'd by God's name,
And I leave them where they are, for I know that
    wheresoe'er I go,
Others will punctually come for ever and ever.

49

And as to you Death, and you bitter hug of mortality, it
    is idle to try to alarm me.

To his work without flinching the accoucheur comes,
I see the elder-hand pressing receiving supporting,
I recline by the sills of the exquisite flexible doors,
And mark the outlet, and mark the relief and escape.

And as to you Corpse I think you are good manure, but
    that does not offend me,
I smell the white roses sweet-scented and growing,
I reach to the leafy lips, I reach to the polish'd breasts of
    melons.

And as to you Life I reckon you are the leavings of many
    deaths,
(No doubt I have died myself ten thousand times before.)

I hear you whispering there O stars of heaven,
O suns—O grass of graves—O perpetual transfers and
    promotions,
If you do not say any thing how can I say any thing?

Of the turbid pool that lies in the autumn forest,
Of the moon that descends the steeps of the soughing
    twilight,
Toss, sparkles of day and dusk—toss on the black stems
    that decay in the muck,
Toss to the moaning gibberish of the dry limbs.

I ascend from the moon, I ascend from the night,
I perceive that the ghastly glimmer is noonday
    sunbeams reflected,
And debouch to the steady and central from the
    offspring great or small.

50

There is that in me—I do not know what it is—but I
know it is in me.

Wrench'd and sweaty—calm and cool then my body
becomes,
I sleep—I sleep long.

I do not know it—it is without name—it is a word
unsaid,
It is not in any dictionary, utterance, symbol.

Something it swings on more than the earth I
swing on,
To it the creation is the friend whose embracing
awakes me.

Perhaps I might tell more. Outlines! I plead for my
brothers and sisters.

Do you see O my brothers and sisters?
It is not chaos or death—it is form, union, plan—it is
eternal life—it is Happiness.

51

The past and present wilt—I have fill'd them, emptied
them,
And proceed to fill my next fold of the future.

Listener up there! what have you to confide to me?
Look in my face while I snuff the sidle of evening,

(Talk honestly, no one else hears you, and I stay only a
    minute longer.)

Do I contradict myself?
Very well then I contradict myself,
(I am large, I contain multitudes.)

I concentrate toward them that are nigh, I wait on the
    door-slab.

Who has done his day's work? who will soonest be
    through with his supper?
Who wishes to walk with me?

Will you speak before I am gone? will you prove already
    too late?

52

The spotted hawk swoops by and accuses me, he
    complains of my gab and my loitering.

I too am not a bit tamed, I too am untranslatable,
I sound my barbaric yawp over the roofs of the world.

The last scud of day holds back for me,
It flings my likeness after the rest and true as any on the
    shadow'd wilds,
It coaxes me to the vapor and the dusk.

I depart as air, I shake my white locks at the runaway
    sun,
I effuse my flesh in eddies, and drift it in lacy jags.

I bequeath myself to the dirt to grow from the grass
    I love,
If you want me again look for me under your boot-soles.

You will hardly know who I am or what I mean,
But I shall be good health to you nevertheless,
And filter and fibre your blood.

Failing to fetch me at first keep encouraged,
Missing me one place search another,
I stop somewhere waiting for you.

[The Sleepers]

I wander all night in my vision,
Stepping with light feet . . . . swiftly and noiselessly
    stepping and stopping,
Bending with open eyes over the shut eyes of sleepers;
Wandering and confused . . . . lost to myself . . . .
    ill-assorted . . . . contradictory,
Pausing and gazing and bending and stopping.

How solemn they look there, stretched and still;
How quiet they breathe, the little children in their
    cradles.

The wretched features of ennuyees, the white features
    of corpses, the livid faces of drunkards, the sick-
    gray faces of onanists,
The gashed bodies on battlefields, the insane in their
    strong-doored rooms, the sacred idiots,
The newborn emerging from gates and the dying
    emerging from gates,
The night pervades them and enfolds them.

The married couple sleep calmly in their bed, he with
    his palm on the hip of the wife, and she with her
    palm on the hip of the husband,
The sisters sleep lovingly side by side in their bed,
The men sleep lovingly side by side in theirs,
And the mother sleeps with her little child carefully
    wrapped.

The blind sleep, and the deaf and dumb sleep,
The prisoner sleeps well in the prison . . . . the
      runaway son sleeps,
The murderer that is to be hung next day . . . . how
      does he sleep?
And the murdered person . . . . how does he sleep?

The female that loves unrequited sleeps,
And the male that loves unrequited sleeps;
The head of the moneymaker that plotted all day sleeps,
And the enraged and treacherous dispositions sleep.

I stand with drooping eyes by the worstsuffering and
      restless,
I pass my hands soothingly to and fro a few inches from
      them;
The restless sink in their beds . . . . they fitfully sleep.

The earth recedes from me into the night,
I saw that it was beautiful . . . . and I see that what is
      not the earth is beautiful.

I go from bedside to bedside . . . . I sleep close with the
      other sleepers, each in turn;
I dream in my dream all the dreams of the other
      dreamers,
And I become the other dreamers.

I am a dance . . . . Play up there! the fit is whirling
      me fast.

I am the everlaughing . . . . it is new moon and twilight,
I see the hiding of douceurs . . . . I see nimble ghosts
    whichever way I look,
Cache and cache again deep in the ground and sea, and
    where it is neither ground or sea.

Well do they do their jobs, those journeymen divine,
Only from me can they hide nothing and would not if
    they could;
I reckon I am their boss, and they make me a pet
    besides,
And surround me, and lead me and run ahead when
    I walk,
And lift their cunning covers and signify me with
    stretched arms, and resume the way;
Onward we move, a gay gang of blackguards with
    mirthshouting music and wildflapping pennants
    of joy.

I am the actor and the actress . . . . the voter . . the
    politician,
The emigrant and the exile . . the criminal that stood in
    the box,
He who has been famous, and he who shall be famous
    after today,
The stammerer . . . . the wellformed person . . the
    wasted or feeble person.

I am she who adorned herself and folded her hair
    expectantly,
My truant lover has come and it is dark.

Double yourself and receive me darkness,
Receive me and my lover too . . . . he will not let me go
without him.

I roll myself upon you as upon a bed . . . . I resign
myself to the dusk.

He whom I call answers me and takes the place of
my lover,
He rises with me silently from the bed.

Darkness you are gentler than my lover . . . . his flesh
was sweaty and panting,
I feel the hot moisture yet that he left me.

My hands are spread forth . . I pass them in all
directions,
I would sound up the shadowy shore to which you are
journeying.

Be careful, darkness . . . . already, what was it
touched me?
I thought my lover had gone . . . . else darkness and he
are one,
I hear the heart-beat . . . . I follow . . I fade away.

O hotcheeked and blushing! O foolish hectic!
O for pity's sake, no one must see me now! . . . . my
clothes were stolen while I was abed,
Now I am thrust forth, where shall I run?

Pier that I saw dimly last night when I looked from the
      windows,
Pier out from the main, let me catch myself with you
      and stay . . . . I will not chafe you;
I feel ashamed to go naked about the world,
And am curious to know where my feet stand . . . . and
      what is this flooding me, childhood or
      manhood . . . . and the hunger that crosses the
      bridge between.

The cloth laps a first sweet eating and drinking,
Laps life-swelling yolks . . . . laps ear of rose-corn,
      milky and just ripened:
The white teeth stay, and the boss-tooth advances in
      darkness,
And liquor is spilled on lips and bosoms by touching
      glasses, and the best liquor afterward.

I descend my western course . . . . my sinews are
      flaccid,
Perfume and youth course through me, and I am
      their wake.

It is my face yellow and wrinkled instead of the old
      woman's,
I sit low in a strawbottom chair and carefully darn my
      grandson's stockings.

It is I too . . . . the sleepless widow looking out on the
      winter midnight,
I see the sparkles of starshine on the icy and pallid earth.

A shroud I see—and I am the shroud . . . . I wrap a
    body and lie in the coffin;
It is dark here underground . . . . it is not evil or pain
    here . . . . it is blank here, for reasons.

It seems to me that everything in the light and air ought
    to be happy;
Whoever is not in his coffin and the dark grave, let him
    know he has enough.

I see a beautiful gigantic swimmer swimming naked
    through the eddies of the sea,
His brown hair lies close and even to his head . . . . he
    strikes out with courageous arms . . . . he urges
    himself with his legs.

I see his white body . . . . I see his undaunted eyes;
I hate the swift-running eddies that would dash him
    headforemost on the rocks.

What are you doing you ruffianly red-trickled waves?
Will you kill the courageous giant? Will you kill him in
    the prime of his middle age?

Steady and long he struggles;
He is baffled and banged and bruised . . . . he holds out
    while his strength holds out,
The slapping eddies are spotted with his blood . . . .
    they bear him away . . . . they roll him and swing
    him and turn him:

His beautiful body is borne in the circling eddies . . . .
    it is continually bruised on rocks,
Swiftly and out of sight is borne the brave corpse.

I turn but do not extricate myself;
Confused . . . . a pastreading . . . . another, but with
    darkness yet.

The beach is cut by the razory ice-wind . . . . the
    wreck-guns sound,
The tempest lulls and the moon comes floundering
    through the drifts.

I look where the ship helplessly heads end on . . . .
    I hear the burst as she strikes . . I hear the howls of
    dismay . . . . they grow fainter and fainter.

I cannot aid with my wringing fingers;
I can but rush to the surf and let it drench me and freeze
    upon me.

I search with the crowd . . . . not one of the company is
    washed to us alive;
In the morning I help pick up the dead and lay them in
    rows in a barn.

Now of the old war-days . . the defeat at Brooklyn;
Washington stands inside the lines . . he stands on the
    entrenched hills amid a crowd of officers,
His face is cold and damp . . . . he cannot repress the
    weeping drops . . . . he lifts the glass perpetually to

his eyes . . . . the color is blanched from his
cheeks,
He sees the slaughter of the southern braves confided to
him by their parents.

The same at last and at last when peace is declared,
He stands in the room of the old tavern . . . . the
wellbeloved soldiers all pass through,
The officers speechless and slow draw near in their
turns,
The chief encircles their necks with his arm and kisses
them on the cheek,
He kisses lightly the wet cheeks one after another . . . .
he shakes hands and bids goodbye to the army.

Now I tell what my mother told me today as we sat at
dinner together,
Of when she was a nearly grown girl living home with
her parents on the old homestead.

A red squaw came one breakfasttime to the old
homestead,
On her back she carried a bundle of rushes for
rushbottoming chairs;
Her hair straight shiny coarse black and profuse
halfenveloped her face,
Her step was free and elastic . . . . her voice sounded
exquisitely as she spoke.

My mother looked in delight and amazement at the
stranger,

She looked at the beauty of her tallborne face and full
and pliant limbs,
The more she looked upon her she loved her,
Never before had she seen such wonderful beauty and
purity;
She made her sit on a bench by the jamb of the
fireplace . . . . she cooked food for her,
She had no work to give her but she gave her
remembrance and fondness.

The red squaw staid all the forenoon, and toward the
middle of the afternoon she went away;
O my mother was loth to have her go away,
All the week she thought of her . . . . she watched for
her many a month,
She remembered her many a winter and many a
summer,
But the red squaw never came nor was heard of there
again.

Now Lucifer was not dead . . . . or if he was I am his
sorrowful terrible heir;
I have been wronged . . . . I am oppressed . . . . I hate
him that oppresses me,
I will either destroy him, or he shall release me.

Damn him! how he does defile me,
How he informs against my brother and sister and takes
pay for their blood,
How he laughs when I look down the bend after the
steamboat that carries away my woman.

Now the vast dusk bulk that is the whale's bulk . . . . it
   seems mine,
Warily, sportsman! though I lie so sleepy and sluggish,
   my tap is death.

A show of the summer softness . . . . a contact of
   something unseen . . . . an amour of the light
   and air;
I am jealous and overwhelmed with friendliness,
And will go gallivant with the light and the air myself,
And have an unseen something to be in contact with
   them also.

O love and summer! you are in the dreams and in me,
Autumn and winter are in the dreams . . . . the farmer
   goes with his thrift,
The droves and crops increase . . . . the barns are
   wellfilled.

Elements merge in the night . . . . ships make tacks in
   the dreams . . . . the sailor sails . . . . the exile
   returns home,
The fugitive returns unharmed . . . . the immigrant is
   back beyond months and years;
The poor Irishman lives in the simple house of his
   childhood, with the wellknown neighbors and
   faces,
They warmly welcome him . . . . he is barefoot
   again . . . . he forgets he is welloff;
The Dutchman voyages home, and the Scotchman and
   Welchman voyage home . . and the native of the
   Mediterranean voyages home;

To every port of England and France and Spain enter
    wellfilled ships;
The Swiss foots it toward his hills . . . . the Prussian
    goes his way, and the Hungarian his way, and the
    Pole goes his way,
The Swede returns, and the Dane and Norwegian return.

The homeward bound and the outward bound,
The beautiful lost swimmer, the ennuyee, the onanist,
    the female that loves unrequited, the moneymaker,
The actor and actress . . those through with their parts
    and those waiting to commence,
The affectionate boy, the husband and wife, the voter,
    the nominee that is chosen and the nominee that
    has failed,
The great already known, and the great anytime after to
    day,
The stammerer, the sick, the perfectformed, the
    homely,
The criminal that stood in the box, the judge that sat
    and sentenced him, the fluent lawyers, the jury, the
    audience,
The laugher and weeper, the dancer, the midnight
    widow, the red squaw,
The consumptive, the erysipalite, the idiot, he that is
    wronged,
The antipodes, and every one between this and them in
    the dark,
I swear they are averaged now . . . . one is no better
    than the other,
The night and sleep have likened them and restored
    them.

I swear they are all beautiful,
Every one that sleeps is beautiful . . . . every thing in
    the dim night is beautiful,
The wildest and bloodiest is over and all is peace.

Peace is always beautiful,
The myth of heaven indicates peace and night.

The myth of heaven indicates the soul;
The soul is always beautiful . . . . it appears more or it
    appears less . . . . it comes or lags behind,
It comes from its embowered garden and looks
    pleasantly on itself and encloses the world;
Perfect and clean the genitals previously jetting, and
    perfect and clean the womb cohering,
The head wellgrown and proportioned and plumb, and
    the bowels and joints proportioned and plumb.

The soul is always beautiful,
The universe is duly in order . . . . every thing is in its
    place,
What is arrived is in its place, and what waits is in its
    place;
The twisted skull waits . . . . the watery or rotten blood
    waits,
The child of the glutton or venerealee waits long, and
    the child of the drunkard waits long, and the
    drunkard himself waits long,
The sleepers that lived and died wait . . . . the far
    advanced are to go on in their turns, and the far
    behind are to go on in their turns,

The diverse shall be no less diverse, but they shall flow
and unite . . . . they unite now.

The sleepers are very beautiful as they lie unclothed,
They flow hand in hand over the whole earth from east
to west as they lie unclothed;
The Asiatic and African are hand in hand . . . . the
European and American are hand in hand,
Learned and unlearned are hand in hand . . and male
and female are hand in hand;
The bare arm of the girl crosses the bare breast of her
lover . . . . they press close without lust . . . . his
lips press her neck,
The father holds his grown or ungrown son in his arms
with measureless love . . . . and the son holds the
father in his arms with measureless love,
The white hair of the mother shines on the white wrist
of the daughter,
The breath of the boy goes with the breath of the
man . . . . friend is inarmed by friend,
The scholar kisses the teacher and the teacher kisses the
scholar . . . . the wronged is made right,
The call of the slave is one with the master's call . . and
the master salutes the slave,
The felon steps forth from the prison . . . . the insane
becomes sane . . . . the suffering of sick persons is
relieved,
The sweatings and fevers stop . . the throat that was
unsound is sound . . the lungs of the consumptive
are resumed . . the poor distressed head is free,
The joints of the rheumatic move as smoothly as ever,
and smoother than ever,

Stiflings and passages open . . . . the paralysed become
    supple,
The swelled and convulsed and congested awake to
    themselves in condition,
They pass the invigoration of the night and the
    chemistry of the night and awake.

I too pass from the night;
I stay awhile away O night, but I return to you again
    and love you;
Why should I be afraid to trust myself to you?
I am not afraid . . . . I have been well brought forward
    by you;
I love the rich running day, but I do not desert her in
    whom I lay so long;
I know not how I came of you, and I know not where I
    go with you . . . . but I know I came well and shall
    go well.

I will stop only a time with the night . . . . and rise
    betimes.

I will duly pass the day O my mother and duly return
    to you;
Not you will yield forth the dawn again more surely
    than you will yield forth me again,
Not the womb yields the babe in its time more surely
    than I shall be yielded from you in my time.

Crossing Brooklyn Ferry

1

Flood-tide below me! I see you face to face!
Clouds of the west—sun there half an hour high—I see
　　you also face to face.

Crowds of men and women attired in the usual
　　costumes, how curious you are to me!
On the ferry-boats the hundreds and hundreds that
　　cross, returning home, are more curious to me than
　　you suppose,
And you that shall cross from shore to shore years hence
　　are more to me, and more in my meditations, than
　　you might suppose.

2

The impalpable sustenance of me from all things at all
　　hours of the day,
The simple, compact, well-join'd scheme, myself
　　disintegrated, every one disintegrated yet part of the
　　scheme,
The similitudes of the past and those of the future,
The glories strung like beads on my smallest sights and
　　hearings, on the walk in the street and the passage
　　over the river,
The current rushing so swiftly and swimming with me
　　far away,

The others that are to follow me, the ties between me
    and them,
The certainty of others, the life, love, sight, hearing of
    others.

Others will enter the gates of the ferry and cross from
    shore to shore,
Others will watch the run of the flood-tide,
Others will see the shipping of Manhattan north and
    west, and the heights of Brooklyn to the south
    and east,
Others will see the islands large and small;
Fifty years hence, others will see them as they cross,
    the sun half an hour high,
A hundred years hence, or ever so many hundred years
    hence, others will see them,
Will enjoy the sunset, the pouring-in of the flood-tide,
    the falling-back to the sea of the ebb-tide.

3

It avails not, time nor place—distance avails not,
I am with you, you men and women of a generation, or
    ever so many generations hence,
Just as you feel when you look on the river and sky, so I
    felt,
Just as any of you is one of a living crowd, I was one of a
    crowd,
Just as you are refresh'd by the gladness of the river and
    the bright flow, I was refresh'd,
Just as you stand and lean on the rail, yet hurry with the
    swift current, I stood yet was hurried,

Just as you look on the numberless masts of ships and
the thick-stemm'd pipes of steamboats, I look'd.

I too many and many a time cross'd the river of old,
Watched the Twelfth-month sea-gulls, saw them high in
the air floating with motionless wings, oscillating
their bodies,
Saw how the glistening yellow lit up parts of their
bodies and left the rest in strong shadow,
Saw the slow-wheeling circles and the gradual edging
toward the south,
Saw the reflection of the summer sky in the water,
Had my eyes dazzled by the shimmering track of beams,
Look'd at the fine centrifugal spokes of light round the
shape of my head in the sunlit water,
Look'd on the haze on the hills southward and south-
westward,
Look'd on the vapor as it flew in fleeces tinged with
violet,
Look'd toward the lower bay to notice the vessels
arriving,
Saw their approach, saw aboard those that were
near me,
Saw the white sails of schooners and sloops, saw the
ships at anchor,
The sailors at work in the rigging or out astride the
spars,
The round masts, the swinging motion of the hulls,
the slender serpentine pennants,
The large and small steamers in motion, the pilots in
their pilot-houses,

The white wake left by the passage, the quick tremulous
    whirl of the wheels,
The flags of all nations, the falling of them at sunset,
The scallop-edged waves in the twilight, the ladled
    cups, the frolicsome crests and glistening,
The stretch afar growing dimmer and dimmer, the gray
    walls of the granite storehouses by the docks,
On the river the shadowy group, the big steam-tug
    closely flank'd on each side by the barges, the
    hay-boat, the belated lighter,
On the neighboring shore the fires from the foundry
    chimneys burning high and glaringly into the
    night,
Casting their flicker of black contrasted with wild red
    and yellow light over the tops of houses, and down
    into the clefts of streets.

4

These and all else were to me the same as they are to
    you,
I loved well those cities, loved well the stately and rapid
    river,
The men and women I saw were all near to me,
Others the same—others who look back on me because
    I look'd forward to them,
(The time will come, though I stop here to-day and
    to-night.)

5

What is it then between us?
What is the count of the scores or hundreds of years
    between us?

Whatever it is, it avails not—distance avails not, and
      place avails not,
I too lived, Brooklyn of ample hills was mine,
I too walk'd the streets of Manhattan island, and bathed
      in the waters around it,
I too felt the curious abrupt questionings stir within me,
In the day among crowds of people sometimes they
      came upon me,
In my walks home late at night or as I lay in my bed
      they came upon me,
I too had been struck from the float forever held in
      solution,
I too had receiv'd identity by my body,
That I was I knew was of my body, and what I should be
      I knew I should be of my body.

6

It is not upon you alone the dark patches fall,
The dark threw its patches down upon me also,
The best I had done seem'd to me blank and suspicious,
My great thoughts as I supposed them, were they not in
      reality meagre?
Nor is it you alone who know what it is to be evil,
I am he who knew what it was to be evil,
I too knitted the old knot of contrariety,
Blabb'd, blush'd, resented, lied, stole, grudg'd,
Had guile, anger, lust, hot wishes I dared not speak,
Was wayward, vain, greedy, shallow, sly, cowardly,
      malignant,
The wolf, the snake, the hog, not wanting in me,
The cheating look, the frivolous word, the adulterous
      wish, not wanting,

Refusals, hates, postponements, meanness, laziness,
    none of these wanting,
Was one with the rest, the days and haps of the rest,
Was call'd by my nighest name by clear loud voices of
    young men as they saw me approaching or
    passing,
Felt their arms on my neck as I stood, or the negligent
    leaning of their flesh against me as I sat,
Saw many I loved in the street or ferry-boat or public
    assembly, yet never told them a word,
Lived the same life with the rest, the same old laughing,
    gnawing, sleeping,
Play'd the part that still looks back on the actor or
    actress,
The same old role, the role that is what we make it,
    as great as we like,
Or as small as we like, or both great and small.

7

Closer yet I approach you,
What thought you have of me now, I had as much of
    you—I laid in my stores in advance,
I consider'd long and seriously of you before you
    were born.

Who was to know what should come home to me?
Who knows but I am enjoying this?
Who knows, for all the distance, but I am as good as
    looking at you now, for all you cannot see me?

8

Ah, what can ever be more stately and admirable to me
than mast-hemm'd Manhattan?
River and sunset and scallop-edg'd waves of flood-tide?
The sea-gulls oscillating their bodies, the hay-boat in
the twilight, and the belated lighter?
What gods can exceed these that clasp me by the hand,
and with voices I love call me promptly and loudly
by my nighest name as I approach?
What is more subtle than this which ties me to the
woman or man that looks in my face?
Which fuses me into you now, and pours my meaning
into you?

We understand then do we not?
What I promis'd without mentioning it, have you not
accepted?
What the study could not teach—what the preaching
could not accomplish is accomplish'd, is it not?

9

Flow on, river! flow with the flood-tide, and ebb with
the ebb-tide!
Frolic on, crested and scallop-edg'd waves!
Gorgeous clouds of the sunset! drench with your
splendor me, or the men and women generations
after me!
Cross from shore to shore, countless crowds of
passengers!
Stand up, tall masts of Mannahatta! stand up, beautiful
hills of Brooklyn!

Throb, baffled and curious brain! throw out questions
and answers!
Suspend here and everywhere, eternal float of solution!
Gaze, loving and thirsting eyes, in the house or street or
public assembly!
Sound out, voices of young men! loudly and musically
call me by my nighest name!
Live, old life! play the part that looks back on the actor
or actress!
Play the old role, the role that is great or small
according as one makes it!
Consider, you who peruse me, whether I may not in
unknown ways be looking upon you;
Be firm, rail over the river, to support those who lean
idly, yet haste with the hasting current;
Fly on, sea-birds! fly sideways, or wheel in large circles
high in the air;
Receive the summer sky, you water, and faithfully hold
it till all downcast eyes have time to take it
from you!
Diverge, fine spokes of light, from the shape of my
head, or any one's head, in the sunlit water!
Come on, ships from the lower bay! pass up or down,
white-sail'd schooners, sloops, lighters!
Flaunt away, flags of all nations! be duly lower'd at
sunset!
Burn high your fires, foundry chimneys! cast black
shadows at nightfall! cast red and yellow light over
the tops of the houses!
Appearances, now or henceforth, indicate what you are,
You necessary film, continue to envelop the soul,

About my body for me, and your body for you, be hung
    out divinest aromas,
Thrive, cities—bring your freight, bring your shows,
    ample and sufficient rivers,
Expand, being than which none else is perhaps more
    spiritual,
Keep your places, objects than which none else is more
    lasting.

You have waited, you always wait, you dumb, beautiful
    ministers,
We receive you with free sense at last, and are insatiate
    henceforward,
Not you any more shall be able to foil us, or withhold
    yourselves from us,
We use you, and do not cast you aside—we plant you
    permanently within us,
We fathom you not—we love you—there is perfection
    in you also,
You furnish your parts toward eternity,
Great or small, you furnish your parts toward the soul.

Out of the Cradle Endlessly Rocking

Out of the cradle endlessly rocking,
Out of the mocking-bird's throat, the musical shuttle,
Out of the Ninth-month midnight,
Over the sterile sands and the fields beyond, where the
    child leaving his bed wander'd alone, bareheaded,
    barefoot,

Down from the shower'd halo,
Up from the mystic play of shadows twining and
    twisting as if they were alive,
Out from the patches of briers and blackberries,
From the memories of the bird that chanted to me,
From your memories sad brother, from the fitful risings
    and fallings I heard,
From under that yellow half-moon late-risen and
    swollen as if with tears,
From those beginning notes of yearning and love there
    in the mist,
From the thousand responses of my heart never to
    cease,
From the myriad thence-arous'd words,
From the word stronger and more delicious than any,
From such as now they start the scene revisiting,
As a flock, twittering, rising, or overhead passing,
Borne hither, ere all eludes me, hurriedly,
A man, yet by these tears a little boy again,
Throwing myself on the sand, confronting the waves,
I, chanter of pains and joys, uniter of here and hereafter,
Taking all hints to use them, but swiftly leaping beyond
    them,
A reminiscence sing.

Once Paumanok,
When the lilac-scent was in the air and Fifth-month
    grass was growing,
Up this seashore in some briers,
Two feather'd guests from Alabama, two together,

And their nest, and four light-green eggs spotted with
      brown,
And every day the he-bird to and fro near at hand,
And every day the she-bird crouch'd on her nest, silent,
      with bright eyes,
And every day I, a curious boy, never too close, never
      disturbing them,
Cautiously peering, absorbing, translating.

Shine! shine! shine!
Pour down your warmth, great sun!
While we bask, we two together.

Two together!
Winds blow south, or winds blow north,
Day come white, or night come black,
Home, or rivers and mountains from home,
Singing all time, minding no time,
While we two keep together.

Till of a sudden,
May-be kill'd, unknown to her mate,
One forenoon the she-bird crouch'd not on the nest,
Nor return'd that afternoon, nor the next,
Nor ever appear'd again.

And thenceforward all summer in the sound of the sea,
And at night under the full of the moon in calmer
      weather,
Over the hoarse surging of the sea,

Or flitting from brier to brier by day,
I saw, I heard at intervals the remaining one, the
      he-bird,
The solitary guest from Alabama.

Blow! blow! blow!
Blow up sea-winds along Paumanok's shore;
I wait and I wait till you blow my mate to me.

Yes, when the stars glisten'd,
All night long on the prong of a moss-scallop'd stake,
Down almost amid the slapping waves,
Sat the lone singer wonderful causing tears.

He call'd on his mate,
He pour'd forth the meanings which I of all men know.

Yes my brother I know,
The rest might not, but I have treasur'd every note,
For more than once dimly down to the beach gliding,
Silent, avoiding the moonbeams, blending myself with
      the shadows,
Recalling now the obscure shapes, the echoes, the
      sounds and sights after their sorts,
The white arms out in the breakers tirelessly tossing,
I, with bare feet, a child, the wind wafting my hair,
Listen'd long and long.

Listen'd to keep, to sing, now translating the notes,
Following you my brother.

Soothe! soothe! soothe!
Close on its wave soothes the wave behind,
And again another behind embracing and lapping, every one
    close,
But my love soothes not me, not me.

Low hangs the moon, it rose late,
It is lagging—O I think it is heavy with love, with love.

O madly the sea pushes upon the land,
With love, with love.

O night! do I not see my love fluttering out among the
    breakers?
What is that little black thing I see there in the white?

Loud! loud! loud!
Loud I call to you, my love!

High and clear I shoot my voice over the waves,
Surely you must know who is here, is here,
You must know who I am, my love.

Low-hanging moon!
What is that dusky spot in your brown yellow?
O it is the shape, the shape of my mate!
O moon do not keep her from me any longer.

Land! land! O land!
Whichever way I turn, O I think you could give me my mate
    back again if you only would,
For I am almost sure I see her dimly whichever way I look.

O rising stars!
Perhaps the one I want so much will rise, will rise with some
      of you.

O throat! O trembling throat!
Sound clearer through the atmosphere!
Pierce the woods, the earth,
Somewhere listening to catch you must be the one I want.

Shake out carols!
Solitary here, the night's carols!
Carols of lonesome love! death's carols!
Carols under that lagging, yellow, waning moon!
O under that moon where she droops almost down into
      the sea!
O reckless despairing carols.

But soft! sink low!
Soft! let me just murmur,
And do you wait a moment you husky-nois'd sea,
For I believe I heard my mate responding to me,
So faint, I must be still, be still to listen,
But not altogether still, for then she might not come
      immediately to me.

Hither my love!
Here I am! here!
With this just-sustain'd note I announce myself to you,
This gentle call is for you my love, for you.

Do not be decoy'd elsewhere,
That is the whistle of the wind, it is not my voice,

That is the fluttering, the fluttering of the spray,
Those are the shadows of leaves.

O darkness! O in vain!
O I am very sick and sorrowful.

O brown halo in the sky near the moon, drooping upon
*   the sea!*
O troubled reflection in the sea!
O throat! O throbbing heart!
And I singing uselessly, uselessly all the night.

O past! O happy life! O songs of joy!
In the air, in the woods, over fields,
Loved! loved! loved! loved! loved!
But my mate no more, no more with me!
We two together no more.

The aria sinking,
All else continuing, the stars shining,
The winds blowing, the notes of the bird continuous
    echoing,
With angry moans the fierce old mother incessantly
    moaning,
On the sands of Paumanok's shore gray and rustling,
The yellow half-moon enlarged, sagging down,
    drooping, the face of the sea almost touching,
The boy ecstatic, with his bare feet the waves, with his
    hair the atmosphere dallying,
The love in the heart long pent, now loose, now at last
    tumultuously bursting,

The aria's meaning, the ears, the soul, swiftly
    depositing,
The strange tears down the cheeks coursing,
The colloquy there, the trio, each uttering,
The undertone, the savage old mother incessantly
    crying,
To the boy's soul's questions sullenly timing, some
    drown'd secret hissing,
To the outsetting bard.

Demon or bird! (said the boy's soul,)
Is it indeed toward your mate you sing? or is it really
    to me?
For I, that was a child, my tongue's use sleeping, now
    I have heard you,
Now in a moment I know what I am for, I awake,
And already a thousand singers, a thousand songs,
    clearer, louder and more sorrowful than yours,
A thousand warbling echoes have started to life within
    me, never to die.

O you singer solitary, singing by yourself, projecting
    me,
O solitary me listening, never more shall I cease
    perpetuating you,
Never more shall I escape, never more the
    reverberations,
Never more the cries of unsatisfied love be absent
    from me,
Never again leave me to be the peaceful child I was
    before what there in the night,
By the sea under the yellow and sagging moon,

The messenger there arous'd, the fire, the sweet hell
    within,
The unknown want, the destiny of me.

O give me the clew! (it lurks in the night here
    somewhere,)
O if I am to have so much, let me have more!

A word then, (for I will conquer it,)
The word final, superior to all,
Subtle, sent up—what is it?—I listen;
Are you whispering it, and have been all the time, you
    seawaves?
Is that it from your liquid rims and wet sands?

Whereto answering, the sea,
Delaying not, hurrying not,
Whisper'd me through the night, and very plainly
    before daybreak,
Lisp'd to me the low and delicious word death,
And again death, death, death, death,
Hissing melodious, neither like the bird nor like my
    arous'd child's heart,
But edging near as privately for me rustling at my feet,
Creeping thence steadily up to my ears and laving me
    softly all over,
Death, death, death, death, death.

Which I do not forget,
But fuse the song of my dusky demon and brother,
That he sang to me in the moonlight on Paumanok's
    gray beach,
With the thousand responsive songs at random,

My own songs awaked from that hour,
And with them the key, the word up from the waves,
The word of the sweetest song and all songs,
That strong and delicious word which, creeping to
    my feet,
(Or like some old crone rocking the cradle, swathed in
    sweet garments, bending aside,)
The sea whisper'd me.

As I Ebb'd with the Ocean of Life

1

As I ebb'd with the ocean of life,
As I wended the shores I know,
As I walk'd where the ripples continually wash you
    Paumanok,
Where they rustle up hoarse and sibilant,
Where the fierce old mother endlessly cries for her
    castaways,
I musing late in the autumn day, gazing off southward,
Held by this electric self out of the pride of which
    I utter poems,
Was seiz'd by the spirit that trails in the lines underfoot,
The rim, the sediment that stands for all the water and
    all the land of the globe.

Fascinated, my eyes reverting from the south, dropt, to
    follow those slender windrows,
Chaff, straw, splinters of wood, weeds, and the sea-gluten,

Scum, scales from shining rocks, leaves of salt-lettuce,
    left by the tide,
Miles walking, the sound of breaking waves the other
    side of me,
Paumanok there and then as I thought the old thought
    of likenesses,
These you presented to me you fish-shaped island,
As I wended the shores I know,
As I walk'd with that electric self seeking types.

2

As I wend to the shores I know not,
As I list to the dirge, the voices of men and women
    wreck'd,
As I inhale the impalpable breezes that set in upon me,
As the ocean so mysterious rolls toward me closer and
    closer,
I too but signify at the utmost a little wash'd-up drift,
A few sands and dead leaves to gather,
Gather, and merge myself as part of the sands and drift.

O baffled, balk'd, bent to the very earth,
Oppress'd with myself that I have dared to open my
    mouth,
Aware now that amid all that blab whose echoes recoil
    upon me I have not once had the least idea who or
    what I am,
But that before all my arrogant poems the real Me
    stands yet untouch'd, untold, altogether unreach'd,
Withdrawn far, mocking me with mock-congratulatory
    signs and bows,

With peals of distant ironical laughter at every word
    I have written,
Pointing in silence to these songs, and then to the sand
    beneath.

I perceive I have not really understood any thing, not a
    single object, and that no man ever can,
Nature here in sight of the sea taking advantage of me
    to dart upon me and sting me,
Because I have dared to open my mouth to sing at all.

3

You oceans both, I close with you,
We murmur alike reproachfully rolling sands and drift,
    knowing not why,
These little shreds indeed standing for you and me
    and all.

You friable shore with trails of debris,
You fish-shaped island, I take what is underfoot,
What is yours is mine my father.

I too Paumanok,
I too have bubbled up, floated the measureless float, and
    been wash'd on your shores,
I too am but a trail of drift and debris,
I too leave little wrecks upon you, you fish-shaped island.

I throw myself upon your breast my father,
I cling to you so that you cannot unloose me,
I hold you so firm till you answer me something.

Kiss me my father,
Touch me with your lips as I touch those I love,
Breathe to me while I hold you close the secret of the
　　　murmuring I envy.

4

Ebb, ocean of life, (the flow will return,)
Cease not your moaning you fierce old mother,
Endlessly cry for your castaways, but fear not, deny
　　　not me,
Rustle not up so hoarse and angry against my feet as
　　　I touch you or gather from you.

I mean tenderly by you and all,
I gather for myself and for this phantom looking down
　　　where we lead, and following me and mine.

Me and mine, loose windrows, little corpses,
Froth, snowy white, and bubbles,
(See, from my dead lips the ooze exuding at last,
See, the prismatic colors glistening and rolling,)
Tufts of straw, sands, fragments,
Buoy'd hither from many moods, one contradicting
　　　another,
From the storm, the long calm, the darkness, the swell,
Musing, pondering, a breath, a briny tear, a dab of
　　　liquid or soil,
Up just as much out of fathomless workings fermented
　　　and thrown,
A limp blossom or two, torn, just as much over waves
　　　floating, drifted at random,

Just as much for us that sobbing dirge of Nature,
Just as much whence we come that blare of the cloud-
    trumpets,
We, capricious, brought hither we know not whence,
    spread out before you,
You up there walking or sitting,
Whoever you are, we too lie in drifts at your feet.

When Lilacs Last in the Dooryard Bloom'd

1

When lilacs last in the dooryard bloom'd,
And the great star early droop'd in the western sky in
    the night,
I mourn'd, and yet shall mourn with ever-returning
    spring.

Ever-returning spring, trinity sure to me you bring,
Lilac blooming perennial and drooping star in the west,
And thought of him I love.

2

O powerful western fallen star!
O shades of night—O moody, tearful night!
O great star disappear'd—O the black murk that hides
    the star!
O cruel hands that hold me powerless—O helpless soul
    of me!
O harsh surrounding cloud that will not free my soul.

In the dooryard fronting an old farm-house near the
     white-wash'd palings,
Stands the lilac-bush tall-growing with heart-shaped
     leaves of rich green,
With many a pointed blossom rising delicate, with the
     perfume strong I love,
With every leaf a miracle—and from this bush in the
     dooryard,
With delicate-color'd blossoms and heart-shaped leaves
     of rich green,
A sprig with its flower I break.

4

In the swamp in secluded recesses,
A shy and hidden bird is warbling a song.

Solitary the thrush,
The hermit withdrawn to himself, avoiding the
     settlements,
Sings by himself a song.

Song of the bleeding throat,
Death's outlet song of life, (for well dear brother I know,
If thou was not granted to sing thou would'st surely die.)

5

Over the breast of the spring, the land, amid cities,
Amid lanes and through old woods, where lately the
     violets peep'd from the ground, spotting the gray
     debris,

Amid the grass in the fields each side of the lanes,
     passing the endless grass,
Passing the yellow-spear'd wheat, every grain from its
     shroud in the dark-brown fields uprisen,
Passing the apple-tree blows of white and pink in the
     orchards,
Carrying a corpse to where it shall rest in the grave,
Night and day journeys a coffin.

6

Coffin that passes through lanes and streets,
Through day and night with the great cloud darkening
     the land,
With the pomp of the inloop'd flags with the cities
     draped in black,
With the show of the States themselves as of
     crape-veil'd women standing,
With processions long and winding and the flambeaus
     of the night,
With the countless torches lit, with the silent sea of
     faces and the unbared heads,
With the waiting depot, the arriving coffin, and the
     sombre faces,
With dirges through the night, with the thousand voices
     rising strong and solemn,
With all the mournful voices of the dirges pour'd
     around the coffin,
The dim-lit churches and the shuddering organs—
     where amid these you journey,
With the tolling tolling bells' perpetual clang,
Here, coffin that slowly passes,
I give you my sprig of lilac.

7

(Nor for you, for one alone,
Blossoms and branches green to coffins all I bring,
For fresh as the morning, thus would I chant a song for
    you O sane and sacred death.

All over bouquets of roses,
O death, I cover you over with roses and early lilies,
But mostly and now the lilac that blooms the first,
Copious I break, I break the sprigs from the bushes,
With loaded arms I come, pouring for you,
For you and the coffins all of you O death.)

8

O western orb sailing the heaven,
Now I know what you must have meant as a month
    since I walk'd,
As I walk'd in silence the transparent shadowy
    night,
As I saw you had something to tell as you bent to me
    night after night,
As you droop'd from the sky low down as if to my side,
    (while the other stars all look'd on,)
As we wander'd together the solemn night, (for
    something I know not what kept me from sleep,)
As the night advanced, and I saw on the rim of the west
    how full you were of woe,
As I stood on the rising ground in the breeze in the cool
    transparent night,
As I watch'd where you pass'd and was lost in the
    netherward black of the night,

As my soul in its trouble dissatisfied sank, as where you
    sad orb,
Concluded, dropt in the night, and was gone.

9

Sing on there in the swamp,
O singer bashful and tender, I hear your notes, I hear
    your call,
I hear, I come presently, I understand you,
But a moment I linger, for the lustrous star has
    detain'd me,
The star my departing comrade holds and detains me.

10

O how shall I warble myself for the dead one there
    I loved?
And how shall I deck my song for the large sweet soul
    that has gone?
And what shall my perfume be for the grave of him
    I love?

Sea-winds blown from east and west,
Blown from the Eastern sea and blown from the
    Western sea, till there on the prairies meeting,
These and with these and the breath of my chant,
I'll perfume the grave of him I love.

11

O what shall I hang on the chamber walls?
And what shall the pictures be that I hang on the walls,
To adorn the burial-house of him I love?

Pictures of growing spring and farms and homes,
With the Fourth-month eve at sundown, and the gray
    smoke lucid and bright,
With floods of the yellow gold of the gorgeous,
    indolent, sinking sun, burning, expanding the air,
With the fresh sweet herbage under foot, and the pale
    green leaves of the trees prolific,
In the distance the flowing glaze, the breast of the river,
    with a wind-dapple here and there,
With ranging hills on the banks, with many a line
    against the sky, and shadows,
And the city at hand with dwellings so dense, and stacks
    of chimneys,
And all the scenes of life and the workshops, and the
    workmen homeward returning.

12

Lo, body and soul—this land,
My own Manhattan with spires, and the sparkling and
    hurrying tides, and the ships,
The varied and ample land, the South and the North in
    the light, Ohio's shores and flashing Missouri,
And ever the far-spreading prairies cover'd with grass
    and corn.

Lo, the most excellent sun so calm and haughty,
The violet and purple morn with just-felt breezes,
The gentle soft-born measureless light,
The miracle spreading bathing all, the fulfill'd noon,
The coming eve delicious, the welcome night and
    the stars,
Over my cities shining all, enveloping man and land.

13

Sing on, sing on you gray-brown bird,
Sing from the swamps, the recesses, pour your chant
      from the bushes,
Limitless out of the dusk, out of the cedars and pines.

Sing on dearest brother, warble your reedy song,
Loud human song, with voice of uttermost woe.

O liquid and free and tender!
O wild and loose to my soul—O wondrous singer!
You only I hear—yet the star holds me, (but will soon
      depart,)
Yet the lilac with mastering odor holds me.

14

Now while I sat in the day and look'd forth,
In the close of the day with its light and the fields of
      spring, and the farmers preparing their crops,
In the large unconscious scenery of my land with its
      lakes and forests,
In the heavenly aerial beauty, (after the perturb'd winds
      and storms,)
Under the arching heavens of the afternoon swift
      passing, and the voices of children and women,
The many-moving sea-tides, and I saw the ships how
      they sail'd,
And the summer approaching with richness, and the
      fields all busy with labor,
And the infinite separate houses, how they all went on,
      each with its meals and minutia of daily usages,

And the streets how their throbbings throbb'd, and the
      cities pent—lo, then and there,
Falling upon them all and among them all, enveloping
      me with the rest,
Appear'd the cloud, appear'd the long black trail,
And I knew death, its thought, and the sacred
      knowledge of death.

Then with the knowledge of death as walking one
      side of me,
And the thought of death close-walking the other side
      of me,
And I in the middle as with companions, and as holding
      the hands of companions,
I fled forth to the hiding receiving night that talks not,
Down to the shores of the water, the path by the swamp
      in the dimness,
To the solemn shadowy cedars and ghostly pines so still.

And the singer so shy to the rest receiv'd me,
The gray-brown bird I know receiv'd us comrades
      three,
And he sang the carol of death, and a verse for him I love.

From deep secluded recesses,
From the fragrant cedars and the ghostly pines so still,
Came the carol of the bird.

And the charm of the carol rapt me,
As I held as if by their hands my comrades in the night,
And the voice of my spirit tallied the song of the bird.

Come lovely and soothing death,
Undulate round the world, serenely arriving, arriving,
In the day, in the night, to all, to each,
Sooner or later delicate death.

Prais'd be the fathomless universe,
For life and joy, and for objects and knowledge curious,
And for love, sweet love—but praise! praise! praise!
For the sure-enwinding arms of cool-enfolding death.

Dark mother always gliding near with soft feet,
Have none chanted for thee a chant of fullest welcome?
Then I chant it for thee, I glorify thee above all,
I bring thee a song that when thou must indeed come,
        come unfalteringly.

Approach strong deliveress,
When it is so, when thou hast taken them I joyously sing
        the dead,
Lost in the loving floating ocean of thee,
Laved in the flood of thy bliss O death.

From me to thee glad serenades,
Dances for thee I propose saluting thee, adornments and
        feastings for thee,
And the sights of the open landscape and the high-spread sky
        are fitting,
And life and the fields, and the huge and thoughtful night.

The night in silence under many a star,
The ocean shore and the husky whispering wave whose voice
        I know,

And the soul turning to thee O vast and well-veil'd death,
And the body gratefully nestling close to thee.

Over the tree-tops I float thee a song,
Over the rising and sinking waves, over the myriad fields and
    the prairies wide,
Over the dense-pack'd cities all and the teeming wharves
    and ways,
I float this carol with joy, with joy to thee O death.

15

To the tally of my soul,
Loud and strong kept up the gray-brown bird,
With pure deliberate notes spreading filling the night.

Loud in the pines and cedars dim,
Clear in the freshness moist and the swamp-perfume,
And I with my comrades there in the night.

While my sight that was bound in my eyes unclosed,
As to long panoramas of visions.

And I saw askant the armies,
I saw as in noiseless dreams hundreds of battle-flags,
Borne through the smoke of the battles and pierc'd with
    missiles I saw them,
And carried hither and yon through the smoke, and torn
    and bloody,
And at last but a few shreds left on the staffs, (and all in
    silence,)
And the staffs all splinter'd and broken.

I saw battle-corpses, myriads of them,
And the white skeletons of young men, I saw them,
I saw the debris and debris of all the slain soldiers of
    the war,
But I saw they were not as was thought,
They themselves were fully at rest, they suffer'd not,
The living remain'd and suffer'd, the mother suffer'd,
And the wife and the child and the musing comrade
    suffer'd,
And the armies that remain'd suffer'd.

16

Passing the visions, passing the night,
Passing, unloosing the hold of my comrades' hands,
Passing the song of the hermit bird and the tallying
    song of my soul,
Victorious song, death's outlet song, yet varying
    ever-altering song,
As low and wailing, yet clear the notes, rising and
    falling, flooding the night,
Sadly sinking and fainting, as warning and warning,
    and yet again bursting with joy,
Covering the earth and filling the spread of the heaven,
As that powerful psalm in the night I heard from
    recesses,
Passing, I leave thee lilac with heart-shaped leaves,
I leave thee there in the door-yard, blooming, returning
    with spring.

I cease from my song for thee,
From my gaze on thee in the west, fronting the west,
    communing with thee,
O comrade lustrous with silver face in the night.

Yet each to keep and all, retrievements out of the night,
The song, the wondrous chant of the gray-brown bird,
And the tallying chant, the echo arous'd in my soul,
With the lustrous and drooping star with the
    countenance full of woe,
With the holders holding my hand nearing the call of
    the bird,
Comrades mine and I in the midst, and their memory
    ever to keep, for the dead I loved so well,
For the sweetest, wisest soul of all my days and lands—
    and this for his dear sake,
Lilac and star and bird twined with the chant of my
    soul,
There in the fragrant pines and the cedars dusk
    and dim.

IV

Poets to Come

Poets to come! orators, singers, musicians to come!
Not to-day is to justify me and answer what I am for,
But you, a new brood, native, athletic, continental,
     greater than before known,
Arouse! for you must justify me.

I myself but write one or two indicative words for the
     future,
I but advance a moment only to wheel and hurry back in
     the darkness.

I am a man who, sauntering along without fully
     stopping, turns a casual look upon you and then
     averts his face,
Leaving it to you to prove and define it,
Expecting the main things from you.

To the Garden the World

To the garden the world anew ascending,
Potent mates, daughters, sons, preluding,
The love, the life of their bodies, meaning and being,
Curious here behold my resurrection after slumber,
The revolving cycles in their wide sweep having
     brought me again,

Amorous, mature, all beautiful to me, all wondrous,
My limbs and the quivering fire that ever plays through
     them, for reasons, most wondrous,
Existing I peer and penetrate still,
Content with the present, content with the past,
By my side or back of me Eve following,
Or in front, and I following her just the same.

From Pent-up Aching Rivers

From pent-up aching rivers,
From that of myself without which I were nothing,
From what I am determin'd to make illustrious, even if
     I stand sole among men,
From my own voice resonant, singing the phallus,
Singing the song of procreation,
Singing the need of superb children and therein superb
     grown people,
Singing the muscular urge and the blending,
Singing the bedfellow's song, (O resistless yearning!
O for any and each the body correlative attracting!
O for you whoever you are your correlative body! O it,
     more than all else, you delighting!)
From the hungry gnaw that eats me night and day,
From native moments, from bashful pains, singing
     them,
Seeking something yet unfound though I have diligently
     sought it many a long year,
Singing the true song of the soul fitful at random,
Renascent with grossest Nature or among animals,

Of that, of them and what goes with them my poems
      informing,
Of the smell of apples and lemons, of the pairing
      of birds,
Of the wet of woods, of the lapping of waves,
Of the mad pushes of waves upon the land, I them
      chanting,
The overture lightly sounding, the strain anticipating,
The welcome nearness, the sight of the perfect body,
The swimmer swimming naked in the bath, or
      motionless on his back lying and floating,
The female form approaching, I pensive, love-flesh
      tremulous aching,
The divine list for myself or you or for any one making,
The face, the limbs, the index from head to foot, and
      what it arouses,
The mystic deliria, the madness amorous, the utter
      abandonment,
(Hark close and still what I now whisper to you,
I love you, O you entirely possess me,
O that you and I escape from the rest and go utterly off,
      free and lawless,
Two hawks in the air, two fishes swimming in the sea
      not more lawless than we;)
The furious storm through me careering, I passionately
      trembling.
The oath of the inseparableness of two together, of the
      woman that loves me and whom I love more than
      my life, that oath swearing,
(O I willingly stake all for you,
O let me be lost if it must be so!
O you and I! what is it to us what the rest do or think?

What is all else to us? only that we enjoy each other and
        exhaust each other if it must be so;)
From the master, the pilot I yield the vessel to,
The general commanding me, commanding all, from
        him permission taking,
From time the programme hastening, (I have loiter'd
        too long as it is,)
From sex, from the warp and from the woof,
From privacy, from frequent repinings alone,
From plenty of persons near and yet the right person
        not near,
From the soft sliding of hands over me and thrusting of
        fingers through my hair and beard,
From the long sustain'd kiss upon the mouth or bosom,
From the close pressure that makes me or any man
        drunk, fainting with excess,
From what the divine husband knows, from the work of
        fatherhood,
From exultation, victory and relief, from the bedfellow's
        embrace in the night,
From the act-poems of eyes, hands, hips and bosoms,
From the cling of the trembling arm,
From the bending curve and the clinch,
From side by side the pliant coverlet off-throwing,
From the one so unwilling to have me leave, and me just
        as unwilling to leave,
(Yet a moment O tender waiter, and I return,)
From the hour of shining stars and dropping dews,
From the night a moment I emerging flitting out,
Celebrate you act divine and you children prepared for,
And you stalwart loins.

I Sing the Body Electric

1

I sing the body electric,
The armies of those I love engirth me and I engirth
    them,
They will not let me off till I go with them, respond
    to them,
And discorrupt them, and charge them full with the
    charge of the soul.

Was it doubted that those who corrupt their own bodies
    conceal themselves?
And if those who defile the living are as bad as they who
    defile the dead?
And if the body does not do fully as much as the soul?
And if the body were not the soul, what is the soul?

2

The love of the body of man or woman balks account,
    the body itself balks account,
That of the male is perfect, and that of the female is
    perfect.

The expression of the face balks account,
But the expression of a well-made man appears not only
    in his face,
It is in his limbs and joints also, it is curiously in the
    joints of his hips and wrists,

It is in his walk, the carriage of his neck, the flex of his
    waist and knees, dress does not hide him,
The strong sweet quality he has strikes through the
    cotton and broadcloth,
To see him pass conveys as much as the best poem,
    perhaps more,
You linger to see his back, and the back of his neck and
    shoulder-side.

The sprawl and fulness of babes, the bosoms and heads
    of women, the folds of their dress, their style as we
    pass in the street, the contour of their shape
    downwards,
The swimmer naked in the swimming-bath, seen as he
    swims through the transparent green-shine, or lies
    with his face up and rolls silently to and fro in the
    heave of the water,
The bending forward and backward of rowers in row-
    boats, the horseman in his saddle,
Girls, mothers, house-keepers, in all their performances,
The group of laborers seated at noon-time with their
    open dinner-kettles, and their wives waiting,
The female soothing a child, the farmer's daughter in
    the garden or cow-yard,
The young fellow hoeing corn, the sleigh-driver driving
    his six horses through the crowd,
The wrestle of wrestlers, two apprentice-boys, quite
    grown, lusty, good-natured, native-born, out on the
    vacant lot at sundown after work,
The coats and caps thrown down, the embrace of love
    and resistance,

The upper-hold and under-hold, the hair rumpled over
and blinding the eyes;
The march of firemen in their own costumes, the play
of masculine muscle through clean-setting trowsers
and waist-straps,
The slow return from the fire, the pause when the bell
strikes suddenly again, and the listening on the
alert,
The natural, perfect, varied attitudes, the bent head, the
curv'd neck and the counting;
Such-like I love—I loosen myself, pass freely, am at the
mother's breast with the little child,
Swim with the swimmers, wrestle with wrestlers, march
in line with the firemen, and pause, listen, count.

3

I knew a man, a common farmer, the father of five sons,
And in them the fathers of sons, and in them the fathers
of sons.
This man was of wonderful vigor, calmness, beauty of
person,
The shape of his head, the pale yellow and white of his
hair and beard, the immeasurable meaning of his
black eyes, the richness and breadth of his
manners,
These I used to go and visit him to see, he was wise also,
He was six feet tall, he was over eighty years old, his
sons were massive, clean, bearded, tan-faced,
handsome,
They and his daughters loved him, all who saw him
loved him,

They did not love him by allowance, they loved him
      with personal love,
He drank water only, the blood show'd like scarlet
      through the clear-brown skin of his face,
He was a frequent gunner and fisher, he sail'd his boat
      himself, he had a fine one presented to him by a
      ship-joiner, he had fowling-pieces presented to him
      by men that loved him,
When he went with his five sons and many grand-sons
      to hunt or fish, you would pick him out as the most
      beautiful and vigorous of the gang,
You would wish long and long to be with him, you
      would wish to sit by him in the boat that you and
      he might touch each other.

4

I have perceiv'd that to be with those I like is enough,
To stop in company with the rest at evening is
      enough,
To be surrounded by beautiful, curious, breathing,
      laughing flesh is enough,
To pass among them or touch any one, or rest my arm
      ever so lightly round his or her neck for a moment,
      what is this then?
I do not ask any more delight, I swim in it as in a sea.

There is something in staying close to men and women
      and looking on them, and in the contact and odor
      of them, that pleases the soul well,
All things please the soul, but these please the soul well.

This is the female form,
A divine nimbus exhales from it from head to foot,
It attracts with fierce undeniable attraction,
I am drawn by its breath as if I were no more than a
     helpless vapor, all falls aside but myself and it,
Books, art, religion, time, the visible and solid earth,
     and what was expected of heaven or fear'd of hell,
     are now consumed,
Mad filaments, ungovernable shoots play out of it, the
     response likewise ungovernable,
Hair, bosom, hips, bend of legs, negligent falling hands
     all diffused, mine too diffused,
Ebb stung by the flow and flow stung by the ebb,
     love-flesh swelling and deliciously aching,
Limitless limpid jets of love hot and enormous, quivering
     jelly of love, white-blow and delirious juice,
Bridegroom night of love working surely and softly into
     the prostrate dawn,
Undulating into the willing and yielding day,
Lost in the cleave of the clasping and sweet-flesh'd day.

This the nucleus—after the child is born of woman,
     man is born of woman,
This the bath of birth, this the merge of small and large,
     and the outlet again.

Be not ashamed women, your privilege encloses the
     rest, and is the exit of the rest,
You are the gates of the body, and you are the gates of
     the soul.

The female contains all qualities and tempers them,
She is in her place and moves with perfect balance,
She is all things duly veil'd, she is both passive and
    active,
She is to conceive daughters as well as sons, and sons as
    well as daughters.

As I see my soul reflected in Nature,
As I see through a mist, One with inexpressible
    completeness, sanity, beauty,
See the bent head and arms folded over the breast, the
    Female I see.

6

The male is not less the soul nor more, he too is in his
    place,
He too is all qualities, he is action and power,
The flush of the known universe is in him,
Scorn becomes him well, and appetite and defiance
    become him well,
The wildest largest passions, bliss that is utmost,
    sorrow that is utmost become him well, pride is
    for him,
The full-spread pride of man is calming and excellent to
    the soul,
Knowledge becomes him, he likes it always, he brings
    every thing to the test of himself,
Whatever the survey, whatever the sea and the sail he
    strikes soundings at last only here,
(Where else does he strike soundings except here?)

The man's body is sacred and the woman's body is sacred,
No matter who it is, it is sacred—is it the meanest one
in the laborers' gang?
Is it one of the dull-faced immigrants just landed on the
wharf?
Each belongs here or anywhere just as much as the
well-off, just as much as you,
Each has his or her place in the procession.

(All is a procession,
The universe is a procession with measured and perfect
motion.)

Do you know so much yourself that you call the
meanest ignorant?
Do you suppose you have a right to a good sight, and he
or she has no right to a sight?
Do you think matter has cohered together from its
diffuse float, and the soil is on the surface, and
water runs and vegetation sprouts,
For you only, and not for him and her?

7

A man's body at auction,
(For before the war I often go to the slave-mart and
watch the sale,)
I help the auctioneer, the sloven does not half know his
business.

Gentlemen look on this wonder,
Whatever the bids of the bidders they cannot be high
        enough for it,
For it the globe lay preparing quintillions of years
        without one animal or plant,
For it the revolving cycles truly and steadily roll'd.

In this head the all-baffling brain,
In it and below it the makings of heroes.

Examine these limbs, red, black, or white, they are
        cunning in tendon and nerve,
They shall be stript that you may see them.

Exquisite, senses, life-lit eyes, pluck, volition,
Flakes of breast-muscle, pliant backbone and neck, flesh
        not flabby, good-sized arms and legs,
And wonders within there yet.

Within there runs blood,
The same old blood! the same red-running blood!
There swells and jets a heart, there all passions, desires,
        reachings, aspirations,
(Do you think they are not there because they are not
        express'd in parlors and lecture-rooms?)

This is not only one man, this the father of those who
        shall be fathers in their turns,
In him the start of populous states and rich republics,
Of him countless immortal lives with countless
        embodiments and enjoyments.

How do you know who shall come from the offspring of
     his offspring through the centuries?
(Who might you find you have come from yourself,
     if you could trace back through the centuries?)

8

A woman's body at auction,
She too is not only herself, she is the teeming mother
     of mothers,
She is the bearer of them that shall grow and be mates
     to the mothers.

Have you ever loved the body of a woman?
Have you ever loved the body of a man?
Do you not see that these are exactly the same to all in
     all nations and times all over the earth?

If any thing is sacred the human body is sacred,
And the glory and sweet of a man is the token of
     manhood untainted,
And in man or woman a clean, strong, firm-fibred body,
     is more beautiful than the most beautiful face.

Have you seen the fool that corrupted his own live
     body? or the fool that corrupted her own live body?
For they do not conceal themselves, and cannot conceal
     themselves.

9

O my body! I dare not desert the likes of you in other
     men and women, nor the likes of the parts of you,

I believe the likes of you are to stand or fall with the
        likes of the soul, (and that they are the soul,)
I believe the likes of you shall stand or fall with my
        poems, and that they are my poems,
Man's, woman's, child's, youth's, wife's, husband's,
        mother's, father's, young man's, young woman's
        poems,
Head, neck, hair, ears, drop and tympan of the ears,
Eyes, eye-fringes, iris of the eye, eyebrows, and the
        waking or sleeping of the lids,
Mouth, tongue, lips, teeth, roof of the mouth, jaws, and
        the jaw-hinges,
Nose, nostrils of the nose, and the partition,
Cheeks, temples, forehead, chin, throat, back of the
        neck, neck-slue,
Strong shoulders, manly beard, scapula, hind-shoulders,
        and the ample side-round of the chest,
Upper-arm, armpit, elbow-socket, lower-arm,
        arm-sinews, arm-bones,
Wrist and wrist-joints, hand, palm, knuckles, thumb,
        forefinger, finger-joints, finger-nails,
Broad breast-front, curling hair of the breast,
        breast-bone, breast-side,
Ribs, belly, backbone, joints of the backbone,
Hips, hip-sockets, hip-strength, inward and outward
        round, man-balls, man-root,
Strong set of thighs, well carrying the trunk above,
Leg-fibres, knee, knee-pan, upper-leg, under-leg,
Ankles, instep, foot-ball, toes, toe-joints, the heel;
All attitudes, all the shapeliness, all the belongings of my
        or your body or of any one's body, male or female,

The lung-sponges, the stomach-sac, the bowels sweet
and clean,
The brain in its folds inside the skull-frame,
Sympathies, heart-valves, palate-valves, sexuality,
maternity,
Womanhood, and all that is a woman, and the man that
comes from woman,
The womb, the teats, nipples, breast-milk, tears,
laughter, weeping, love-looks, love-perturbations
and risings,
The voice, articulation, language, whispering, shouting
aloud,
Food, drink, pulse, digestion, sweat, sleep, walking,
swimming,
Poise on the hips, leaping, reclining, embracing,
arm-curving and tightening,
The continual changes of the flex of the mouth, and
around the eyes,
The skin, the sunburnt shade, freckles, hair,
The curious sympathy one feels when feeling with the
hand the naked meat of the body,
The circling rivers the breath, and breathing it in
and out,
The beauty of the waist, and thence of the hips, and
thence downward toward the knees,
The thin red jellies within you or within me, the bones
and the marrow in the bones,
The exquisite realization of health;
O I say these are not the parts and poems of the body
only, but of the soul,
O I say now these are the soul!

A Woman Waits for Me

A woman waits for me, she contains all, nothing is
    lacking,
Yet all were lacking if sex were lacking, or if the
    moisture of the right man were lacking.

Sex contains all, bodies, souls,
Meanings, proofs, purities, delicacies, results,
    promulgations,
Songs, commands, health, pride, the maternal mystery,
    the seminal milk,
All hopes, benefactions, bestowals, all the passions,
    loves, beauties, delights of the earth,
All the governments, judges, gods, follow'd persons of
    the earth,
These are contain'd in sex as parts of itself and
    justifications of itself.

Without shame the man I like knows and avows the
    deliciousness of his sex,
Without shame the woman I like knows and avows hers.

Now I will dismiss myself from impassive women,
I will go stay with her who waits for me, and with those
    women that are warm-blooded and sufficient for me,
I see that they understand me and do not deny me,
I see that they are worthy of me, I will be the robust
    husband of those women.

They are not one jot less than I am,
They are tann'd in the face by shining suns and blowing
    winds,
Their flesh has the old divine suppleness and strength,
They know how to swim, row, ride, wrestle, shoot, run,
    strike, retreat, advance, resist, defend themselves,
They are ultimate in their own right—they are calm,
    clear, well-possess'd of themselves.

I draw you close to me, you women,
I cannot let you go, I would do you good,
I am for you, and you are for me, not only for our own
    sake, but for others' sakes,
Envelop'd in you sleep greater heroes and bards,
They refuse to awake at the touch of any man but me.

It is I, you women, I make my way,
I am stern, acrid, large, undissuadable, but I love you,
I do not hurt you any more than is necessary for you,
I pour the stuff to start sons and daughters fit for these
    States, I press with slow rude muscle,
I brace myself effectually, I listen to no entreaties,
I dare not withdraw till I deposit what has so long
    accumulated within me.

Through you I drain the pent-up rivers of myself,
In you I wrap a thousand onward years,
On you I graft the grafts of the best-beloved of me and
    America,
The drops I distil upon you shall grow fierce and
    athletic girls, new artists, musicians, and singers,

The babes I beget upon you are to beget babes in
their turn,
I shall demand perfect men and women out of my
love-spendings,
I shall expect them to interpenetrate with others, as
I and you interpenetrate now,
I shall count on the fruits of the gushing showers of
them, as I count on the fruits of the gushing
showers I give now,
I shall look for loving crops from the birth, life, death,
immortality, I plant so lovingly now.

Spontaneous Me

Spontaneous me, Nature,
The loving day, the mounting sun, the friend, I am
happy with,
The arm of my friend hanging idly over my shoulder,
The hillside whiten'd with blossoms of the
mountain ash,
The same late in autumn, the hues of red, yellow, drab,
purple, and light and dark green,
The rich coverlet of the grass, animals and birds, the
private untrimm'd bank, the primitive apples, the
pebble-stones,
Beautiful dripping fragments, the negligent list of one
after another as I happen to call them to me or
think of them,
The real poems, (what we call poems being merely
pictures,)

The poems of the privacy of the night, and of men
        like me,
This poem drooping shy and unseen that I always carry,
        and that all men carry,
(Know once for all, avow'd on purpose, wherever are
        men like me, are our lusty lurking masculine
        poems,)
Love-thoughts, love-juice, love-odor, love-yielding,
        love-climbers, and the climbing sap,
Arms and hands of love, lips of love, phallic thumb of
        love, breasts of love, bellies press'd and glued
        together with love,
Earth of chaste love, life that is only life after love,
The body of my love, the body of the woman I love,
        the body of the man, the body of the earth,
Soft forenoon airs that blow from the south-west,
The hairy wild-bee that murmurs and hankers up and
        down, that gripes the full-grown lady-flower,
        curves upon her with amorous firm legs, takes his
        will of her, and holds himself tremulous and tight
        till he is satisfied;
The wet of woods through the early hours,
Two sleepers at night lying close together as they sleep,
        one with an arm slanting down across and below
        the waist of the other,
The smell of apples, aromas from crush'd sage-plant,
        mint, birch-bark,
The boy's longings, the glow and pressure as he confides
        to me what he was dreaming,
The dead leaf whirling its spiral whirl and falling still
        and content to the ground,

The no-form'd stings that sights, people, objects, sting
    me with,
The hubb'd sting of myself, stinging me as much as it
    ever can any one,
The sensitive, orbic, underlapp'd brothers, that only
    privileged feelers may be intimate where they are,
The curious roamer the hand roaming all over the body,
    the bashful withdrawing of flesh where the fingers
    soothingly pause and edge themselves,
The limpid liquid within the young man,
The vex'd corrosion so pensive and so painful,
The torment, the irritable tide that will not be at rest,
The like of the same I feel, the like of the same in
    others,
The young man that flushes and flushes, and the young
    woman that flushes and flushes,
The young man that wakes deep at night, the hot hand
    seeking to repress what would master him,
The mystic amorous night, the strange half-welcome
    pangs, visions, sweats,
The pulse pounding through palms and trembling
    encircling fingers, the young man all color'd, red,
    ashamed, angry;
The souse upon me of my lover the sea, as I lie willing
    and naked,
The merriment of the twin babes that crawl over the
    grass in the sun, the mother never turning her
    vigilant eyes from them,
The walnut-trunk, the walnut-husks, and the ripening
    or ripen'd long-round walnuts,
The continence of vegetables, birds, animals,

The consequent meanness of me should I skulk or find
      myself indecent, while birds and animals never
      once skulk or find themselves indecent,
The great chastity of paternity, to match the great
      chastity of maternity,
The oath of procreation I have sworn, my Adamic and
      fresh daughters,
The greed that eats me day and night with hungry
      gnaw, till I saturate what shall produce boys to fill
      my place when I am through,
The wholesome relief, repose, content,
And this bunch pluck'd at random from myself,
It has done its work—I toss it carelessly to fall where
      it may.

Ages and Ages Returning at Intervals

Ages and ages returning at intervals,
Undestroy'd, wandering immortal,
Lusty, phallic, with the potent original loins, perfectly
      sweet,
I, chanter of Adamic songs,
Through the new garden the West, the great cities
      calling,
Deliriate, thus prelude what is generated, offering these,
      offering myself,
Bathing myself, bathing my songs in Sex,
Offspring of my loins.

O Hymen! O Hymenee!

O hymen! O hymenee! why do you tantalize me thus?
O why sting me for a swift moment only?
Why can you not continue? O why do you now cease?
Is it because if you continued beyond the swift moment
    you would soon certainly kill me?

I Am He that Aches with Love

I am he that aches with amorous love;
Does the earth gravitate? does not all matter, aching,
    attract all matter?
So the body of me to all I meet or know.

Facing West from California's Shores

Facing west from California's shores,
Inquiring, tireless, seeking what is yet unfound,
I, a child, very old, over waves, towards the house of
    maternity, the land of migrations, look afar,
Look off the shores of my Western sea, the circle almost
    circled;
For starting westward from Hindustan, from the vales
    of Kashmere,

From Asia, from the north, from the God, the sage, and
    the hero,
From the south, from the flowery peninsulas and the
    spice islands,
Long having wander'd since, round the earth having
    wander'd,
Now I face home again, very pleas'd and joyous,
(But where is what I started for so long ago?
And why is it yet unfound?)

As Adam Early in the Morning

As Adam early in the morning,
Walking forth from the bower refresh'd with sleep,
Behold me where I pass, hear my voice, approach,
Touch me, touch the palm of your hand to my body as
    I pass,
Be not afraid of my body.

v

In Paths Untrodden

In paths untrodden,
In the growth by margins of pond-waters,
Escaped from the life that exhibits itself,
From all the standards hitherto publish'd, from the
        pleasures, profits, conformities,
Which too long I was offering to feed my soul,
Clear to me now standards not yet publish'd, clear to
        me that my soul,
That the soul of the man I speak for rejoices
        in comrades,
Here by myself away from the clank of the world,
Tallying and talk'd to here by tongues aromatic,
No longer abash'd, (for in this secluded spot I can
        respond as I would not dare elsewhere,)
Strong upon me the life that does not exhibit itself, yet
        contains all the rest,
Resolv'd to sing no songs to-day but those of manly
        attachment,
Projecting them along that substantial life,
Bequeathing hence types of athletic love,
Afternoon this delicious Ninth-month in my
        forty-first year,
I proceed for all who are or have been young men,
To tell the secret of my nights and days,
To celebrate the need of comrades.

Scented Herbage of My Breast

Scented herbage of my breast,
Leaves from you I glean, I write, to be perused best
      afterwards,
Tomb-leaves, body-leaves growing up above me
      above death,
Perennial roots, tall leaves, O the winter shall not freeze
      you delicate leaves,
Every year shall you bloom again, out from where you
      retired you shall emerge again;
O I do not know whether many passing by will discover
      you or inhale your faint odor, but I believe a
      few will;
O slender leaves! O blossoms of my blood! I permit you
      to tell in your own way of the heart that is
      under you,
O I do not know what you mean there underneath
      yourselves, you are not happiness,
You are often more bitter than I can bear, you burn and
      sting me,
Yet you are beautiful to me you faint tinged roots, you
      make me think of death,
Death is beautiful from you, (what indeed is finally
      beautiful except death and love?)
O I think it is not for life I am chanting here my chant
      of lovers, I think it must be for death,
For how calm, how solemn it grows to ascend to the
      atmosphere of lovers,

Death or life I am then indifferent, my soul declines
    to prefer,
(I am not sure but the high soul of lovers welcomes
        death most,)
Indeed O death, I think now these leaves mean precisely
        the same as you mean,
Grow up taller sweet leaves that I may see! grow up out
        of my breast!
Spring away from the conceal'd heart there!
Do not fold yourself so in your pink-tinged roots
        timid leaves!
Do not remain down there so ashamed, herbage of
        my breast!
Come I am determin'd to unbare this broad breast of
        mine, I have long enough stifled and choked;
Emblematic and capricious blades I leave you, now you
        serve me not,
I will say what I have to say by itself,
I will sound myself and comrades only, I will never again
        utter a call only their call,
I will raise with it immortal reverberations through
        the States,
I will give an example to lovers to take permanent shape
        and will through the States,
Through me shall the words be said to make death
        exhilarating,
Give me your tone therefore O death, that I may accord
        with it,
Give me yourself, for I see that you belong to me now
        above all, and are folded inseparably together, you
        love and death are,

Nor will I allow you to balk me any more with what
    I was calling life,
For now it is convey'd to me that you are the purports
    essential,
That you hide in these shifting forms of life, for reasons,
    and that they are mainly for you,
That you beyond them come forth to remain, the
    real reality,
That behind the mask of materials you patiently wait,
    no matter how long,
That you will one day perhaps take control of all,
That you will perhaps dissipate this entire show of
    appearance,
That may-be you are what it is all for, but it does not
    last so very long,
But you will last very long.

Whoever You Are Holding Me Now in Hand

Whoever you are holding me now in hand,
Without one thing all will be useless,
I give you fair warning before you attempt me further,
I am not what you supposed, but far different.

Who is he that would become my follower?
Who would sign himself a candidate for my affections?

The way is suspicious, the result uncertain, perhaps
    destructive,

You would have to give up all else, I alone would expect
      to be your sole and exclusive standard,
Your novitiate would even then be long and exhausting,
The whole past theory of your life and all conformity to
      the lives around you would have to be abandon'd,
Therefore release me now before troubling yourself any
      further, let go your hand from my shoulders,
Put me down and depart on your way.

Or else by stealth in some wood for trial,
Or back of a rock in the open air,
(For in any roof'd room of a house I emerge not, nor
      in company,
And in libraries I lie as one dumb, a gawk, or unborn,
      or dead,)
But just possibly with you on a high hill, first watching
      lest any person for miles around approach unawares,
Or possibly with you sailing at sea, or on the beach of
      the sea or some quiet island,
Here to put your lips upon mine I permit you,
With the comrade's long-dwelling kiss or the new
      husband's kiss,
For I am the new husband and I am the comrade.

Or if you will, thrusting me beneath your clothing,
Where I may feel the throbs of your heart or rest upon
      your hip,
Carry me when you go forth over land or sea;
For thus merely touching you is enough, is best,
And thus touching you would I silently sleep and be
      carried eternally.

But these leaves conning you con at peril,
For these leaves and me you will not understand,
They will elude you at first and still more afterward,
    I will certainly elude you,
Even while you should think you had unquestionably
    caught me, behold!
Already you see I have escaped from you.

For it is not for what I have put into it that I have
    written this book,
Nor is it by reading it you will acquire it,
Nor do those know me best who admire me and
    vauntingly praise me,
Nor will the candidates for my love (unless at most a
    very few) prove victorious,
Nor will my poems do good only, they will do just as
    much evil, perhaps more,
For all is useless without that which you may guess at
    many times and not hit, that which I hinted at;
Therefore release me and depart on your way.

Of the Terrible Doubt of Appearances

Of the terrible doubt of appearances,
Of the uncertainty after all, that we may be deluded,
That may-be reliance and hope are but speculations
    after all,
That may-be identity beyond the grave is a beautiful
    fable only,

May-be the things I perceive, the animals, plants, men,
hills, shining and flowing waters,
The skies of day and night, colors, densities, forms,
may-be these are (as doubtless they are) only
apparitions, and the real something has yet to
be known,
(How often they dart out of themselves as if to
confound me and mock me!
How often I think neither I know, nor any man knows,
aught of them,)
May-be seeming to me what they are (as doubtless they
indeed but seem) as from my present point of view,
and might prove (as of course they would) nought
of what they appear, or nought anyhow, from
entirely changed points of view;
To me these and the like of these are curiously answer'd
by my lovers, my dear friends,
When he whom I love travels with me or sits a long
while holding me by the hand,
When the subtle air, the impalpable, the sense that
words and reason hold not, surround us and
pervade us,
Then I am charged with untold and untellable wisdom,
I am silent, I require nothing further,
I cannot answer the question of appearances or that of
identity beyond the grave,
But I walk or sit indifferent, I am satisfied,
He ahold of my hand has completely satisfied me.

City of Orgies

City of orgies, walks and joys,
City whom that I have lived and sung in your midst will
    one day make you illustrious,
Not the pageants of you, not your shifting tableaus,
    your spectacles, repay me,
Not the interminable rows of your houses, nor the ships
    at the wharves,
Nor the processions in the streets, nor the bright
    windows with goods in them,
Nor to converse with learn'd persons, or bear my share
    in the soiree or feast;
Not those, but as I pass O Manhattan, your frequent
    and swift flash of eyes offering me love,
Offering response to my own—these repay me,
Lovers, continual lovers, only repay me.

I Saw in Louisiana a Live-Oak Growing

I saw in Louisiana a live-oak growing,
All alone stood it and the moss hung down from the
    branches,
Without any companion it grew there uttering joyous
    leaves of dark green,
And its look, rude, unbending, lusty, made me think of
    myself,

But I wonder'd how it could utter joyous leaves standing
  alone there without its friend near, for I knew
  I could not,
And I broke off a twig with a certain number of leaves
  upon it, and twined around it a little moss,
And brought it away, and I have placed it in sight in my
  room,
It is not needed to remind me as of my own dear
  friends,
(For I believe lately I think of little else than of them,)
Yet it remains to me a curious token, it makes me think
  of manly love;
For all that, and though the live-oak glistens there in
  Louisiana solitary in a wide flat space,
Uttering joyous leaves all its life without a friend a lover
  near,
I know very well I could not.

VI

On the Beach at Night

On the beach at night,
Stands a child with her father,
Watching the east, the autumn sky.

Up through the darkness,
While ravening clouds, the burial clouds, in black
    masses spreading,
Lower sullen and fast athwart and down the sky,
Amid a transparent clear belt of ether yet left in the east,
Ascends large and calm the lord-star Jupiter,
And nigh at hand, only a very little above,
Swim the delicate sisters the Pleiades.

From the beach the child holding the hand of her
    father,
Those burial-clouds that lower victorious soon to
    devour all,
Watching, silently weeps.

Weep not, child,
Weep not, my darling,
With these kisses let me remove your tears,
The ravening clouds shall not long be victorious,
They shall not long possess the sky, they devour the
    stars only in apparition,
Jupiter shall emerge, be patient, watch again another
    night, the Pleiades shall emerge,

They are immortal, all those stars both silvery and
    golden shall shine out again,
The great stars and the little ones shall shine out again,
    they endure,
The vast immortal suns and the long-enduring pensive
    moons shall again shine.

Then dearest child mournest thou only for Jupiter?
Considerest thou alone the burial of the stars?

Something there is,
(With my lips soothing thee, adding I whisper,
I give thee the first suggestion, the problem and
    indirection,)
Something there is more immortal even than the stars,
(Many the burials, many the days and night, passing
    away,)
Something that shall endure longer even than lustrous
    Jupiter,
Longer than sun or any revolving satellite,
Or the radiant sisters the Pleiades.

The World Below the Brine

The world below the brine,
Forests at the bottom of the sea, the branches and
    leaves,
Sea-lettuce, vast lichens, strange flowers and seeds, the
    thick tangle, openings, and pink turf,

Different colors, pale gray and green, purple, white, and
 gold, the play of light through the water,
Dumb swimmers there among the rocks, coral, gluten,
 grass, rushes, and the aliment of the swimmers,
Sluggish existences grazing there suspended, or slowly
 crawling close to the bottom,
The sperm-whale at the surface blowing air and spray,
 or disporting with his flukes,
The leaden-eyed shark, the walrus, the turtle, the hairy
 sea-leopard, and the sting-ray,
Passions there, wars, pursuits, tribes, sight in those
 ocean-depths, breathing that thick-breathing air,
 as so many do,
The change thence to the sight here, and to the subtle
 air breathed by beings like us who walk this
 sphere,
The change onward from ours to that of beings who
 walk other spheres.

A Hand-Mirror

Hold it up sternly—see this it sends back, (who is it? is
 it you?)
Outside fair costume, within ashes and filth,
No more a flashing eye, no more a sonorous voice or
 springy step,
Now some slave's eye, voice, hands, step,
A drunkard's breath, unwholesome eater's face,
 venerealee's flesh,

Lungs rotting away piecemeal, stomach sour and
    cankerous,
Joints rheumatic, bowels clogged with abomination,
Blood circulating dark and poisonous streams,
Words babble, hearing and touch callous,
No brain, no heart left, no magnetism of sex;
Such from one look in this looking-glass ere you go
    hence,
Such a result so soon—and from such a beginning!

The Dalliance of the Eagles

Skirting the river road, (my forenoon walk, my rest,)
Skyward in air a sudden muffled sound, the dalliance of
    the eagles,
The rushing amorous contact high in space together,
The clinching interlocking claws, a living, fierce,
    gyrating wheel,
Four beating wings, two beaks, a swirling mass tight
    grappling,
In tumbling turning clustering loops, straight downward
    falling,
Till o'er the river pois'd, the twain yet one, a moment's
    lull,
A motionless still balance in the air, then parting, talons
    loosing,
Upward again on slow-firm pinions slanting, their
    separate diverse flight,
She hers, he his, pursuing.

As Toilsome I Wander'd Virginia's Woods

As toilsome I wander'd Virginia's woods,
To the music of rustling leaves kick'd by my feet, (for
    'twas autumn,)
I mark'd at the foot of a tree the grave of a soldier;
Mortally wounded he and buried on the retreat, (easily
    all could I understand,)
The halt of a mid-day hour, when up! no time to lose—
    yet this sign left,
On a tablet scrawl'd and nail'd on the tree by the grave,
Bold, cautious, true, and my loving comrade.

Long, long I muse, then on my way go wandering,
Many a changeful season to follow, and many a scene
    of life,
Yet at times through changeful season and scene,
    abrupt, alone, or in the crowded street,
Comes before me the unknown soldier's grave, comes
    the inscription rude in Virginia's woods,
Bold, cautious, true, and my loving comrade.

The Wound-Dresser

1

An old man bending I come among new faces,
Years looking backward resuming in answer to children,
Come tell us old man, as from young men and maidens
    that love me,
(Arous'd and angry, I'd thought to beat the alarum, and
    urge relentless war,
But soon my fingers fail'd me, my face droop'd
    and I resign'd myself,
To sit by the wounded and soothe them, or silently
    watch the dead;)
Years hence of these scenes, of these furious passions,
    these chances,
Of unsurpass'd heroes, (was one side so brave? the other
    was equally brave;)
Now be witness again, paint the mightiest armies of
    earth,
Of those armies so rapid so wondrous what saw you to
    tell us?
What stays with you latest and deepest? of curious
    panics,
Of hard-fought engagements or sieges tremendous what
    deepest remains?

O maidens and young men I love and that love me,
What you ask of my days those the strangest and sudden
      your talking recalls,
Soldier alert I arrive after a long march cover'd with
      sweat and dust,
In the nick of time I come, plunge in the fight, loudly
      shout in the rush of successful charge,
Enter the captur'd works—yet lo, like a swift-running
      river they fade,
Pass and are gone they fade—I dwell not on soldiers'
      perils or soldiers' joys,
(Both I remember well—many the hardships, few the
      joys, yet I was content.)

But in silence, in dreams' projections,
While the world of gain and appearance and mirth
      goes on,
So soon what is over forgotten, and waves wash the
      imprints off the sand,
With hinged knees returning I enter the doors, (while
      for you up there,
Whoever you are, follow without noise and be of strong
      heart.)

Bearing the bandages, water and sponge,
Straight and swift to my wounded I go,
Where they lie on the ground after the battle brought in,
Where their priceless blood reddens the grass the
      ground,

Or to the rows of the hospital tent, or under the roof'd
hospital,
To the long rows of cots up and down each side I return,
To each and all one after another I draw near, not one
do I miss,
An attendant follows holding a tray, he carries a
refuse pail,
Soon to be fill'd with clotted rags and blood, emptied,
and fill'd again.

I onward go, I stop,
With hinged knees and steady hand to dress wounds,
I am firm with each, the pangs are sharp yet unavoidable,
One turns to me his appealing eyes—poor boy! I never
knew you,
Yet I think I could not refuse this moment to die for
you, if that would save you.

3

On, on I go, (open doors of time! open hospital doors!)
The crush'd head I dress, (poor crazed hand tear not the
bandage away,)
The neck of the cavalry-man with the bullet through
and through I examine,
Hard the breathing rattles, quite glazed already the eye,
yet life struggles hard,
(Come sweet death! be persuaded O beautiful death!
In mercy come quickly.)

From the stump of the arm, the amputated hand,
I undo the clotted lint, remove the slough, wash off the
matter and blood,

Back on his pillow the soldier bends with curv'd neck
    and side-falling head,
His eyes are closed, his face is pale, he dares not look on
    the bloody stump,
And has not yet look'd on it.

I dress a wound in the side, deep, deep,
But a day or two more, for see the frame all wasted
    and sinking,
And the yellow-blue countenance see.

I dress the perforated shoulder, the foot with the
    bullet-wound,
Cleanse the one with a gnawing and putrid gangrene,
    so sickening, so offensive,
While the attendant stands behind aside me holding the
    tray and pail.

I am faithful, I do not give out,
The fractur'd thigh, the knee, the wound in the
    abdomen,
These and more I dress with impassive hand, (yet deep
    in my breast a fire, a burning flame.)

4

Thus in silence in dreams' projections,
Returning, resuming, I thread my way through the
    hospitals,
The hurt and wounded I pacify with soothing hand,
I sit by the restless all the dark night, some are so
    young,

Some suffer so much, I recall the experience sweet
    and sad,
(Many a soldier's loving arms about this neck have
    cross'd and rested,
Many a soldier's kiss dwells on these bearded lips.)

Reconciliation

Word over all, beautiful as the sky,
Beautiful that war and all its deeds of carnage must in
    time be utterly lost,
That the hands of the sisters Death and Night incessantly
    softly wash again, and ever again, this soil'd world;
For my enemy is dead, a man divine as myself is dead,
I look where he lies white-faced and still in the coffin—I
    draw near,
Bend down and touch lightly with my lips the white face
    in the coffin.

There Was a Child Went Forth

There was a child went forth every day,
And the first object he look'd upon, that object he
    became,
And that object became part of him for the day or a
    certain part of the day,
Or for many years or stretching cycles of years.

The early lilacs became part of this child,
And grass and white and red morning-glories, and white
and red clover, and the song of the phœbe-bird,
And the Third-month lambs and the sow's pink-faint
litter, and the mare's foal and the cow's calf,
And the noisy brood of the barnyard or by the mire of
the pond-side,
And the fish suspending themselves so curiously below
there, and the beautiful curious liquid,
And the water-plants with their graceful flat heads, all
became part of him.

The field-sprouts of Fourth-month and Fifth-month
became part of him,
Winter-grain sprouts and those of the light-yellow corn,
and the esculent roots of the garden,
And the apple-trees cover'd with blossoms and the fruit
afterward, and wood-berries, and the commonest
weeds by the road,
And the old drunkard staggering home from the
outhouse of the tavern whence he had lately risen,
And the schoolmistress that pass'd on her way to the
school,
And the friendly boys that pass'd, and the quarrelsome
boys,
And the tidy and fresh-cheek'd girls, and the barefoot
negro boy and girl,
And all the changes of city and country wherever he
went.

His own parents, he that had father'd him and she that
    had conceiv'd him in her womb and birth'd him,
They gave this child more of themselves than that,
They gave him afterward every day, they became part
    of him.

The mother at home quietly placing the dishes on the
    supper-table,
The mother with mild words, clean her cap and gown, a
    wholesome odor falling off her person and clothes
    as she walks by,
The father, strong, self-sufficient, manly, mean, anger'd,
    unjust,
The blow, the quick loud word, the tight bargain, the
    crafty lure,
The family usages, the language, the company, the
    furniture, the yearning and swelling heart,
Affection that will not be gainsay'd, the sense of what
    is real, the thought if after all it should prove
    unreal,
The doubts of day-time and the doubts of night-time,
    the curious whether and how,
Whether that which appears so is so, or is it all flashes
    and specks?
Men and women crowding fast in the streets, if they are
    not flashes and specks what are they?
The streets themselves and the façades of houses, and
    goods in the windows,
Vehicles, teams, the heavy-plank'd wharves, the huge
    crossing at the ferries,
The village on the highland seen from afar at sunset, the
    river between,

Shadows, aureola and mist, the light falling on roofs and
    gables of white or brown two miles off,
The schooner near by sleepily dropping down the tide,
    the little boat slack-tow'd astern,
The hurrying tumbling waves, quick-broken crests,
    slapping,
The strata of color'd clouds, the long bar of maroon-
    tint away solitary by itself, the spread of purity it
    lies motionless in,
The horizon's edge, the flying sea-crow, the fragrance of
    salt marsh and shore mud,
These became part of that child who went forth every
    day, and who now goes, and will always go forth
    every day.

VII

Chanting the Square Deific

1

Chanting the square deific, out of the One advancing,
    out of the sides,
Out of the old and new, out of the square entirely divine,
Solid, four-sided, (all the sides needed,) from this side
    Jehovah am I,
Old Brahm I, and I Saturnius am;
Not Time affects me—I am Time, old, modern as any,
Unpersuadable, relentless, executing righteous
    judgments,
As the Earth, the Father, the brown old Kronos,
    with laws,
Aged beyond computation, yet ever new, ever with
    those mighty laws rolling,
Relentless I forgive no man—whoever sins dies—I will
    have that man's life;
Therefore let none expect mercy—have the seasons,
    gravitation, the appointed days, mercy? no more
    have I,
But as the seasons and gravitation, and as all the
    appointed days that forgive not,
I dispense from this side judgments inexorable without
    the least remorse.

2

Consolator most mild, the promis'd one advancing,
With gentle hand extended, the mightier God am I,

Foretold by prophets and poets in their most rapt
      prophecies and poems,
From this side, lo! the Lord Christ gazes—lo! Hermes
      I—lo! mine is Hercules' face,
All sorrow, labor, suffering, I, tallying it, absorb in
      myself,
Many times have I been rejected, taunted, put in prison,
      and crucified, and many times shall be again,
All the world have I given up for my dear brothers' and
      sisters' sake, for the soul's sake,
Wending my way through the homes of men, rich or
      poor, with the kiss of affection,
For I am affection, I am the cheer-bringing God, with
      hope and all-enclosing charity,
With indulgent words as to children, with fresh and
      sane words, mine only,
Young and strong I pass knowing well I am destin'd
      myself to an early death;
But my charity has no death—my wisdom dies not,
      neither early nor late,
And my sweet love bequeath'd here and elsewhere
      never dies.

3

Aloof, dissatisfied, plotting revolt,
Comrade of criminals, brother of slaves,
Crafty, despised, a drudge, ignorant,
With sudra face and worn brow, black, but in the depths
      of my heart, proud as any,
Lifted now and always against whoever scorning
      assumes to rule me,

Morose, full of guile, full of reminiscences, brooding,
    with many wiles,
(Though it was thought I was baffled and dispel'd, and
    my wiles done, but that will never be,)
Defiant, I, Satan, still live, still utter words, in new lands
    duly appearing, (and old ones also,)
Permanent here from my side, warlike, equal with any,
    real as any,
Nor time nor change shall ever change me or my
    words.

4

Santa Spirita, breather, life,
Beyond the light, lighter than light,
Beyond the flames of hell, joyous, leaping easily
    above hell,
Beyond Paradise, perfumed solely with mine own
    perfume,
Including all life on earth, touching, including God,
    including Saviour and Satan,
Ethereal, pervading all, (for without me what were all?
    what were God?)
Essence of forms, life of the real identities, permanent,
    positive, (namely the unseen,)
Life of the great round world, the sun and stars, and of
    man, I, the general soul,
Here the square finishing, the solid, I the most
    solid,
Breathe my breath also through these songs.

A Noiseless Patient Spider

A noiseless patient spider,
I mark'd where on a little promontory it stood isolated,
Mark'd how to explore the vacant vast surrounding,
It launch'd forth filament, filament, filament, out of
      itself,
Ever unreeling them, ever tirelessly speeding them.

And you O my soul where you stand,
Surrounded, detached, in measureless oceans of space,
Ceaselessly musing, venturing, throwing, seeking the
      spheres to connect them,
Till the bridge you will need be form'd, till the ductile
      anchor hold,
Till the gossamer thread you fling catch somewhere,
      O my soul.

O Living Always, Always Dying

O living always, always dying!
O the burials of me past and present,
O me while I stride ahead, material, visible, imperious
    as ever;
O me, what I was for years, now dead, (I lament not,
    I am content;)
O to disengage myself from those corpses of me, which
    I turn and look at where I cast them,
To pass on, (O living! always living!) and leave the
    corpses behind.

The Last Invocation

At the last, tenderly,
From the walls of the powerful fortress'd house,
From the clasp of the knitted locks, from the keep of the
    well-closed doors,
Let me be wafted.

Let me glide noiselessly forth;
With the key of softness unlock the locks—with a
    whisper,
Set ope the doors O soul.

Tenderly—be not impatient,
(Strong is your hold O mortal flesh,
Strong is your hold O love.)

A Clear Midnight

This is thy hour O Soul, thy free flight into the wordless,
Away from books, away from art, the day erased, the
    lesson done,
Thee fully forth emerging, silent, gazing, pondering the
    themes thou lovest best,
Night, sleep, death and the stars.

Good-Bye my Fancy

Good-bye my fancy—(I had a word to say,
But 'tis not quite the time—The best of any man's word
    or say,
Is when its proper place arrives—and for its meaning,
I keep mine till the last.)

When the Full-Grown Poet Came

When the full-grown poet came,
Out spake pleased Nature (the round impassive globe,
    with all its shows of day and night,) saying, *He
    is mine;*
But out spake too the Soul of man, proud, jealous and
    unreconciled, *Nay, he is mine alone;*
—Then the full-grown poet stood between the two, and
    took each by the hand;

And to-day and ever so stands, as blender, uniter, tightly
    holding hands,
Which he will never release until he reconciles the two,
And wholly and joyously blends them.

Good-Bye my Fancy!

Good-bye my Fancy!
Farewell dear mate, dear love!
I'm going away, I know not where,
Or to what fortune, or whether I may ever see you again,
So Good-bye my Fancy.

Now for my last—let me look back a moment;
The slower fainter ticking of the clock is in me,
Exit, nightfall, and soon the heart-thud stopping.

Long have we lived, joy'd, caress'd together;
Delightful!—now separation—Good-bye my Fancy.

Yet let me not be too hasty,
Long indeed have we lived, slept, filter'd, become really
    blended into one;
Then if we die we die together, (yes, we'll remain one,)
If we go anywhere we'll go together to meet what
    happens,
May-be we'll be better off and blither, and learn
    something,
May-be it is yourself now really ushering me to the true
    songs, (who knows?)

May-be it is you the mortal knob really undoing,
    turning—so now finally,
Good-bye—and hail! my Fancy.

—————

Respondez! Respondez!
Let every one answer! Let those who sleep be waked!
    Let none evade—not you, any more than others!
(If it really be as is pretended, how much longer must
    we go on with our affectations and sneaking?
Let me bring this to a close—I pronounce openly for a
    new distribution of roles,)
Let that which stood in front go behind! and let that
    which was behind advance to the front and speak!
Let murderers, thieves, bigots, fools, unclean persons,
    offer new propositions!
Let the old propositions be postponed!
Let faces and theories be turned inside out! Let
    meanings be freely criminal, as well as results!
Let there be no suggestion above the suggestion of
    drudgery!
Let none be pointed toward his destination! (Say! do
    you know your destination?)
Let trillions of men and women be mocked with bodies
    and mocked with Souls!
Let the love that waits in them, wait! Let it die, or pass
    still-born to other spheres!
Let the sympathy that waits in every man, wait! or let it
    also pass, a dwarf, to other spheres!

Let contradictions prevail! Let one thing contradict
  another! and let one line of my poems contradict
  another!
Let the people sprawl with yearning aimless hands! Let
  their tongues be broken! Let their eyes be
  discouraged! Let none descend into their hearts
  with the fresh lusciousness of love!
Let the theory of America be management, caste,
  comparison! (Say! what other theory would you?)
Let them that distrust birth and death lead the rest!
  (Say! why shall they not lead you?)
Let the crust of hell be neared and trod on! Let the days
  be darker than the nights! Let slumber bring less
  slumber than waking-time brings!
Let the world never appear to him or her for whom it
  was all made!
Let the heart of the young man exile itself from the
  heart of the old man! and let the heart of the old
  man be exiled from that of the young man!
Let the sun and moon go! Let scenery take the applause
  of the audience! Let there be apathy under the stars!
Let freedom prove no man's inalienable right! Every
  one who can tyrannize, let him tyrannize to his
  satisfaction!
Let none but infidels be countenanced!
Let the eminence of meanness, treachery, sarcasm, hate,
  greed, indecency, impotence, lust, be taken for
  granted above all! Let writers, judges, governments,
  households, religions, philosophies, take such for
  granted above all!
Let the worst men beget children out of the worst
  women!

Let priests still play at immortality!

Let Death be inaugurated!

Let nothing remain upon the earth except the ashes of teachers, artists, moralists, lawyers, and learned and polite persons!

Let him who is without my poems be assassinated!

Let the cow, the horse, the camel, the garden-bee— Let the mud-fish, the lobster, the mussel, eel, the sting-ray, and the grunting pig-fish—Let these, and the like of these, be put on a perfect equality with man and woman!

Let churches accommodate serpents, vermin, and the corpses of those who have died of the most filthy of diseases!

Let marriage slip down among fools, and be for none but fools!

Let men among themselves talk and think obscenely of women! and let women among themselves talk and think obscenely of men!

Let every man doubt every woman! and let every woman trick every man!

Let us all, without missing one, be exposed in public, naked, monthly, at the peril of our lives! Let our bodies be freely handled and examined by whoever chooses!

Let nothing but copies, pictures, statues, reminiscences, elegant works, be permitted to exist upon the earth!

Let the earth desert God, nor let there ever henceforth be mentioned the name of God!

Let there be no God!

Let there be money, business, imports, exports, custom,
   authority, precedents, pallor, dyspepsia, smut,
   ignorance, unbelief!
Let judges and criminals be transposed! Let the
   prison-keepers be put in prison! Let those that
   were prisoners take the keys! (Say! why might they
   not just as well be transposed?)
Let the slaves be masters! Let the masters become
   slaves!
Let the reformers descend from the stands where they
   are forever bawling! Let an idiot or insane person
   appear on each of the stands!
Let the Asiatic, the African, the European, the
   American and the Australian, go armed against the
   murderous stealthiness of each other! Let them
   sleep armed! Let none believe in good-will!
Let there be no unfashionable wisdom! Let such be
   scorned and derided off from the earth!
Let a floating cloud in the sky—Let a wave of the sea—
   Let one glimpse of your eye-sight upon the
   landscape or grass—Let growing mint, spinach,
   onions, tomatoes—Let these be exhibited as shows
   at a great price for admission!
Let all the men of These States stand aside for a few
   smouchers! Let the few seize on what they choose!
   Let the rest gawk, giggle, starve, obey!
Let shadows be furnished with genitals! Let substances
   be deprived of their genitals!
Let there be wealthy and immense cities—but through
   any of them, not a single poet, saviour, knower,
   lover!

Let the infidels of These States laugh all faith away! If
   one man be found who has faith, let the rest set
   upon him! Let them affright faith! Let them
   destroy the power of breeding faith!
Let the she-harlots and the he-harlots be prudent! Let
   them dance on, while seeming lasts! (O seeming!
   seeming! seeming!)
Let the preachers recite creeds! Let them teach only
   what they have been taught!
Let the preachers of creeds never dare to go meditate
   candidly upon the hills, alone, by day or by night!
   (If one ever once dare, he is lost!)
Let insanity have charge of sanity!
Let books take the place of trees, animals, rivers, clouds!
Let the daubed portraits of heroes supersede heroes!
Let the manhood of man never take steps after itself!
   Let it take steps after eunuchs, and after
   consumptive and genteel persons!
Let the white person tread the black person under his
   heel! (Say! which is trodden under heel, after all?)
Let the reflections of the things of the world be studied
   in mirrors! Let the things themselves continue
   unstudied!
Let a man seek pleasure everywhere except in himself!
   Let a woman seek happiness everywhere except in
   herself! (Say! what real happiness have you had one
   single time through your whole life?)
Let the limited years of life do nothing for the limitless
   years of death! (Say! what do you suppose death
   will do, then?)

BIOGRAPHICAL NOTE

Walt Whitman was born May 31, 1819, in West Hills, Huntington Township, New York. He was the son of Louisa Van Velsor and Walter Whitman, a farmer and carpenter; his parents were descended from early settlers on Long Island. The family moved in 1823 to Brooklyn, where Whitman attended public schools until about 1830. He learned the printing trade on the Brooklyn newspapers the *Patriot* and the *Star*, and worked as a printer until 1836. From 1836 to 1838 he taught school on Long Island. He founded and edited the newspaper *The Long-Islander* (1838–39) at Huntington, and worked on the Jamaica *Democrat*, publishing some of his early poetry there. He moved to Manhattan in 1841 and worked as a compositor for *New World*, contributed fiction and journalistic sketches to newspapers and magazines, and published the temperance novel *Franklin Evans; or, The Inebriate* (1842). Returning to Brooklyn, he worked for the *Star* (1845–46) and the *Daily Eagle*, a Democratic Party newspaper (1846–48) from which he was fired for his bias toward the Free-Soil Party. He went to New Orleans where he edited *The Crescent* for three months, then returned to New York and founded and edited *The Brooklyn Freeman* (1848–49) and ran printing, bookselling, and house-building businesses. He published four topical poems in 1850 and in 1855, at his own expense, he published *Leaves of Grass*. From Ralph Waldo Emerson, to whom he had sent a copy, he received a letter of praise. An expanded second edition of *Leaves of Grass* was published the following year. He edited the *Brooklyn Times* from 1857 to 1859. In 1860 he went to Boston to oversee a third, greatly enlarged edition of *Leaves of Grass*. After the outbreak of the Civil War, Whitman visited sick, injured, and wounded soldiers at New York Hospital and the war front in Virginia. He settled in Washington, D.C., and became a volunteer nurse in military hospitals, supporting himself by part-time clerical work in the Army Paymaster's office; he returned to Brooklyn on sick leave in 1864. In Washington a year later, he was appointed to a clerkship at the Department of the Interior and later he worked as a clerk in the Attorney General's office. His poems on the war and its aftermath were published in *Drum-Taps* and *Sequel to Drum-Taps* (both 1865). New editions of *Leaves of Grass* appeared in 1867 and 1870. Whitman's prose was collected in *Democratic Vistas* (1871) and *Memoranda During the War* (1875), and his long poem *Passage to India*, inspired by the opening of the Suez Canal, was published in 1870. In 1873 he suffered a stroke and left Washington for Camden, New Jersey, where he lived for the rest of his life. The 1881 edition of *Leaves of Grass* was reprinted in Philadelphia by Rees Welsh & Co. along with the prose collection *Specimen Days and Collect*. Whitman suffered a second stroke in 1888, the same year that he published the prose collection *November Boughs* and *Complete Poems and Prose*. *Good-Bye my Fancy* and the final, so-called "deathbed" edition of *Leaves of Grass* were published in 1891. He had prepared an edition of his *Complete Prose Works* before his death on March 26, 1892.

NOTE ON THE TEXTS

The texts of the poems in this volume are taken from the final "deathbed" edition of *Leaves of Grass* (Philadelphia, 1891–92), with the exception of the following poems, which are taken from the sources identified below:

"I am your voice—It was tied in you—In me it begins to talk," "The crowds naked in the bath," "There is no word in any tongue": *Leaves of Grass*, edited by Emory Holloway (Garden City, N. Y.: Doubleday & Company, 1926).

"I am the poet of reality," "One touch of a tug of me has unhaltered all my senses but feeling," "Afar in the sky was a nest," "In vain were nails driven through my hands": *The Uncollected Poetry and Prose of Walt Whitman*, Volume II, edited by Emory Holloway (Garden City, N. Y.: Doubleday & Company, 1921). In the text of "One touch of a tug of me has un-haltered all my senses but feeling" printed in the Holloway edition, "wherever" (4.25) is followed by "[wherein?]," indicating a conjecture regarding the word Whitman had crossed out at this point in his manu-script. This volume does not print the "[wherein?]." In the Holloway edition "endure" (5.22) is followed by "(?)"; in this volume, the ques-tion mark is printed without parentheses.

"I wander all night in my vision" [The Sleepers]: *Leaves of Grass* (Brooklyn, 1855).

"Respondez! Respondez!": *Leaves of Grass* (Washington, D.C., 1871)

The following is a list of pages where a stanza break coincides with the foot of the page (except where such breaks are apparent from the regular stanzaic structure of the poem): 11, 12, 13, 15, 17, 18, 19, 22, 23, 24, 25, 34, 35, 36, 37, 39, 40, 42, 44, 47, 50, 53, 59, 60, 61, 62, 63, 65, 66, 68, 70, 71, 74, 75, 77, 79, 80, 81, 82, 83, 84, 85, 86, 87, 88, 91, 95, 96, 97, 98, 99, 103, 105, 112, 120, 121, 128, 134, 137, 139, 140, 154, 155, 156, 160, 175, 192.

NOTES

14.4   entretied]   Cross-braced (a carpentry term).

14.21–23   As the hugging . . . tread,]   In the 1855 *Leaves of Grass* Whitman wrote: "As God comes a loving bedfellow and sleeps at my side all night. . . ."

17.23   Kanuck, Tuckahoe, Congressman, Cuff]   French Canadian, Native American, European American, African American.

28.13   jour printer]   Journeyman printer working for daily wages.

29.7   Wolverine]   Inhabitant of Michigan.

32.17–18   Hoosier, Badger, Buckeye]   Inhabitants of Indiana, Wisconsin, and Ohio respectively.

48.11   fakes]   Coils of ropes.

56.5   life-car]   Life-saving compartment drawn on lines and cables between two ships.

56.28   bull-dances]   Frontier dances involving men, in the absence of female partners.

59.14   seven satellites]   The seven planets (aside from Earth) known in Whitman's day.

63.27–28   'Tis the tale . . . young men.]   Mexican troops captured about 400 men near Goliad on March 20, 1836, most of them volunteers from the southern United States. Having previously decreed that all foreigners captured under arms on Mexican soil would be treated as pirates, Santa Anna ordered their execution, and about 330 of the prisoners were shot on March 27.

65.11 old-time sea-fight] During the Revolutionary War the American warship *Bonhomme Richard*, commanded by John Paul Jones, encountered the British frigate *Serapis*. The battle on September 23, 1779, off the North Sea coast of England was an American victory, although the *Bonhomme Richard* later sank.

75.13–14 trestles of death] Sawhorses placed under a coffin to elevate it.

84.8 chuff] The heel of the hand.

98.21–99.16 O hotcheeked . . . liquor afterward.] These lines were deleted in the 1881 *Leaves of Grass* and subsequent editions.

101.21–102.4 Now of the old war-days . . . by their parents.] The Continental Army was defeated in the Battle of Long Island, August 27, 1776, which was fought in present-day Brooklyn.

102.6 old tavern] Fraunces Tavern in lower Manhattan, where on December 4, 1783, Washington said farewell to his officers.

103.19–104.4 Now Lucifer . . . tap is death.] These lines were subsequently deleted from the poem.

104.10–11 And have . . . them also.] This line was subsequently deleted.

108.22–25 Not you will yield . . . in my time.] These lines were subsequently deleted.

118.25 Paumanok] Long Island.

132.7 Carrying a corpse . . . the grave,] Lincoln's body was brought to Springfield, Illinois, for burial.

200.27 sudra] Hindu lower caste for menial occupations.

204.8 Good-bye] Whitman's note: "Behind a Good-bye there lurks much of the salutation of another beginning—to me, Development, Continuity, Immortality, Transformation, are the chiefest life-meanings of Nature and Humanity, and are the *sine qua non* of all facts, and each fact.

"Why do folks dwell so fondly on the last words, advice, appearance, of the departing? Those last words are not samples of the best, which involve vitality at its full, and balance, and perfect control and scope. But they are valuable beyond measure to confirm and endorse the varied train, facts, theories and faith of the whole preceding life."

INDEX OF TITLES
AND FIRST LINES

AMERICAN POETS PROJECT

EDNA ST. VINCENT MILLAY: SELECTED POEMS
J. D. McClatchy, editor
ISBN 1-931082-35-9 $20.00

———

POETS OF WORLD WAR II
Harvey Shapiro, editor
ISBN 1-931082-33-2 $20.00

———

KARL SHAPIRO: SELECTED POEMS
John Updike, editor
ISBN 1-931082-34-0 $20.00

———

WALT WHITMAN: SELECTED POEMS
Harold Bloom, editor
ISBN 1-931082-32-4 $20.00